t h e

h e a r t
MENDER

Other books by Sally Streib:

Summer of the Shark

Treasures of the Sea

To order additional copies of

The Heart Mender

by

Sally Streib,

call 1-800-765-6955.

Visit us at

www.reviewandherald.com

for information on other Review and Herald® products.

the

heart
MENDER

He had found me—I was treasure.
No matter what else changed, that never would.

sally streib

REVIEW AND HERALD® PUBLISHING ASSOCIATION
HAGERSTOWN, MD 21740

The Review and Herald Publishing Association publishes biblically-based
materials for spiritual, physical, and mental growth and Christian discipleship.

The author assumes full responsibility for the accuracy of all facts and quotations as cited
in this book.

This book was
Edited by Penny Estes Wheeler
Cover design by Trent Truman
Cover photo by photographer/artist Kevin Forest
Interior design by Candy Harvey
Electronic makeup by Shirley M. Bolivar
Typeset: 12/14 Bembo

PRINTED IN U.S.A.

10 09 08 07 06   5 4 3 2 1

R&H Cataloging Service
Streib, Sally Ann, 1943-
     The heart mender: He had found me—I was treasure. No matter what else changed,
that never would.

     1. Religious life.   2. Spiritual life.
3. Women—Religious life.   I. Title

                    248.843

ISBN 10: 0-8280-1890-1
ISBN 13: 978-0-8280-1890-6

DEDICATION

to Martha Willis

She listened! She loved me through troubled, uncertain times, drawing me into her family circle. When she could have remained comfortably at home, she set out with me, traveling hundreds of miles, keeping me encouraged and organized as I learned to deliver week of prayer programs.

She has the wisdom to accept me as I am and the courage to set me straight now and again. I will be forever grateful that in spite of her fear of water and lack of desire to meet up with sharks, she took SCUBA lessons and leaped with me into the deep blue seas of the world.

ACKNOWLEDGMENTS

When the Heart Mender sets to work on a human heart, He uses many human helpers. Thank you, Stephen, David, and Sally. You gave me the courage to set out on an amazing adventure instead of taking the regular, easier road. Thank you, educators, pastors, and women's directors. You invited me to your schools, your churches, and retreats where the love and interaction with students and adults enlivened and blessed me. I send a thank you to my special friends who have gone diving and shelling with me, fanning the flame of my love for the sea into a blazing fire.

Thank you to those of you who hardly knew me yet shared your homes, your funds, and all sorts of gifts, making my journeys from Cayman to Canada easier and safer.

I smile as I think of how my editors, Penny and Jeannette, took my material and shaped it into a book. They did a good job!

And I'm especially grateful to my brother Grover, author of *Nobody's Boy,* for drawing my brothers and sisters together again. We're having a riot of a time getting to know each other again, laughing and crying over our early years, and discussing life's journey after years of separation.

Thank you, Heart Mender, for using each experience, every kind word, and even the smallest gift to make my life—in spite of many challenges—an amazement to myself and others, and for making this book a reality.

CONTENTS

CHAPTER 1 ~ The Search / 13

*We're all searching for something. It takes many forms
and is called many names. But what it is, is love.*

CHAPTER 2 ~ The Discovery / 28

*God doesn't always save us from heartache,
but He can keep us from despair.*

CHAPTER 3 ~ The Fight Against Fear / 44

*I decided not to hate and blame. I had to let go of these
so God could fill me with something better.*

CHAPTER 4 ~ The Choice / 61

*I would not leave Him. Without the sun, the world would be black as
night. Without Jesus, I would walk in darkness.*

CHAPTER 5 ~ Face-to-face With the Heart Mender / 76

*When He won our trust He showed us how to hide in His love
through the storms.*

CHAPTER 6 ~ Listening to the Heart Mender / 92

God is there, but we can't see Him. Our eyes are on other things.

CHAPTER 7 ~ Talking With the Heart Mender / 110

I visualize myself curled up on His lap.

CHAPTER 8 ~ The Gift of a Mended Heart / 122

The Potter knows the person you long to be.

CHAPTER 9 ~ The Response of a Mended Heart / 138

*The wounded heart heals slowly. Nights of agony fade
into mornings of peace.*

PREFACE

This book traces the lives of two women. Both were given up as lost and worthless. Each became beloved by God, valued and fully alive.

Mary* lived in ancient times, walked dusty streets, and drew water from a well. Her search for love crashed on the rocks of false promises leaving her disgraced and brokenhearted. But when her enemies threw her at the feet of Jesus, she found the love of her life, and the healing and acceptance she craved. Thus healed, she poured herself out—a lavish gift—on the broken lives of others.

I am Sally, the second woman. I live today. I fly in jets. I shop the Internet, and I SCUBA dive. My search for love began in childhood,  groping through the darkness of abandonment and fear. Later, I survived shipwreck on the rocks of divorce. Turning from the grasping claws of bitterness, I had to choose to refuse to hate.

At last, determined to learn the truth about a God I'd only glimpsed as a frightened child, I discovered an extravagant love that set me free and catapulted me onto a pathway of adventure.

Dear reader, find yourself within the pages of these women's lives. Their experiences differ widely, yet their pain and fear is shared. Both women suffered shame and loss, pain and panic, yet each made life-changing discoveries. Each found the Heart Mender.

Discover a love that seeps into the wounds of your heart, knitting its fibers together again. Watch it grow into a brilliant joy, leaving you radiant with an inner security and happiness. Then stand amazed as it sets you off on your own adventure designed especially for you by the Heart Mender.

---

*I believe that the woman caught in adultery was Mary Magdalene. After this first encounter with Jesus, Mary became a devoted disciple. In the biblical narrative, found only in the Gospel of John (8:3-11), she is referred to as "a woman." In other places in the Gospel stories Mary Magdalene is also called "a woman" (Luke 7:37). Perhaps John, recognizing this to be an extremely embarrassing situation, chose to tell her story in an anonymous format to protect her reputation.

CHAPTER ONE

The Search

We're all searching for something. It takes many forms
and is called many names. But what it is, is love.

THE ALABASTER BOX

Mary peered through the archway that opened into a cluttered room. She searched the sweaty faces of the guests who lounged on plush couches before tables groaning under a load of figs, dates, fresh-baked bread, and lamb stew. Sounds of dishes clattering together and the hum of mingled voices collided in the heated air.

Where could Jesus be? Had He come to the feast? Mary felt that she must find Him and listen to His words. Her eyes searched the faces of those clustered about the tables and brightened when she saw Jesus reclining on a couch, speaking to Lazarus. When He glanced in her direction, she smiled and edged close to Him, seating herself on the tile floor near His feet where she could hide from the prying eyes of the other guests.

Just to be near Jesus made her heart sing! His words danced again in her memory. "Neither do I condemn you!" Again, joy swelled up within her until she felt like shouting.

Mary longed to talk of this joy with her sister, but Martha was always so busy, darting here and there about the house, robe swirling. She had watched for a chance to speak of her feelings, and even followed Martha as she passed from room to room, snatching up clothing and plumping pillows.

Mary sighed and leaned against the couch. Jesus' musical voice reached out and encircled her. She listened to each word, her finger stroking the silk ribbon that held a precious alabaster box about her neck. She traced the outline of a dove carved into the box and smiled. Her memory took her back three days and placed her in the merchant's booth.

"Sir, I wish to purchase an alabaster box of spikenard for a friend."

"You want alabaster? Spikenard? Humph!" The merchant spat the words out, his full lips curling up into a sneer. "You can't afford such, woman!" He reached toward her with a hairy hand and felt the sleeve of her homespun garment between his fingers, grimacing at its roughness. "Be off with you. I'm a busy man." He brushed her aside as one would a fly.

"Please!" she pleaded. "I've saved so long." She fumbled with the ties on the small leather pouch that hung at her waist beneath her outer garment then dumped its contents onto the table between them.

The merchant's beady eyes darted over the coins. He sucked in his breath, stroking his short, stubby beard. Then he began sorting the money with quick jabs of his fingers. "Three hundred pence. More than a year's wages for the likes of you," he said, prying his eyes from the coins and fastening his gaze upon her.

Without waiting for her to speak, he turned, parted the lavish tapestries that hung at the back of the booth and disappeared. Mary stared with wide eyes at his retreating form. *Run!* her mind screamed. *Run!* But her feet refused to move.

In a moment the curtains jerked apart and the merchant stomped up to the table. He placed a wooden box beside the scattered coins and flipped the top up.

Mary gasped! On deep folds of scarlet silk lay six carved alabaster boxes. *I must have one,* she thought.

"You've enough to buy this one," the merchant said, indicating the smallest box with a jab of his ring-bedecked finger. "That's a good bargain. After all, spikenard is for the rich."

Mary stared at the treasures before her.

"Going to gawk all day, woman?" the merchant grumbled impatiently. He picked up the small box and thrust it toward her.

Mary encircled the box with her fingers and hugged it to herself. She turned away. The sound of coins clinking together followed her as she fled from the dark booth and burst into the sunlight. She shook to rid herself of the stare that clung to her back. It didn't matter. She owned the alabaster box! She searched for the blue ribbon in her pocket, then made a large loop around her neck and tied it to the box. It fell against her breast, hidden by her robe. Only she knew of the precious secret.

Suddenly Jesus' words pushed aside her memories. "I am the Lamb of God," He said, looking deeply into the face of Lazarus. "Soon I will be beaten and nailed to a cross."

Lazarus groaned and glanced around at the others who stared at Jesus.

This can't be! Mary's mind screamed in protest. Jesus is the King, the Messiah. *He can't die!* Her heart pounded beneath her robe and she felt frozen in place. But what if He is right? What if Jesus is about to die?

The presence of a new thought jolted her. Why not anoint Him—now! Why wait until He's dead? As if obeying an inner command, she grasped the box and loosed it from the ribbon. Breaking it open, she poured the ointment over Jesus feet. Tears, long-restrained, cascaded from reservoirs deep inside her and mingled with the ointment. Mary removed the combs from her hair and let it tumble about her shoulders. Then she gathered it in her hands and dried His feet.

A sweet fragrance burst into the room, filling every corner. Conversations stopped. Guests' eyes darted about the room, searching for the source of the wondrous scent. Mary winced when they stopped at her, staring. Suddenly the room erupted with excited voices.

"Look at that!" a woman exclaimed, turning to her companion. "Wait until I tell Deborah!"

"She won't believe it!" came the reply. "Imagine Jesus allowing that woman to touch Him."

"What a waste!" another voice jeered. "The money from that purchase could have fed hundreds."

Each harsh word stabbed into Mary's heart. She trembled, shrinking from the guests in horror. No one understood her gift. No one knew that she just had to thank Him for all He had done—He had forgiven her sin and treated her with respect when no one else did. Would Jesus understand? Or would He rebuke her, too?

The alabaster box fell from her hand onto the floor.

"Let her alone!" Jesus said in a loud voice. "Can't you see what a lovely thing she has done for Me? When I die on the cross you will bring your spices for My dead body, but Mary has brought her gift to Me while I yet live."

He turned from the astonished faces of the guests to look into her eyes. "Thank you, Mary," He said simply. "Your gift of love and gratitude will comfort Me in the terrible days ahead."

Mary gazed at her Savior's face, drinking in His understanding and acceptance. "Wonderful Jesus, I will serve you as long as I live," she whispered. Gathering her robe together and pushing a stray lock of hair behind her ear, she arose and slipped from the room, a beloved woman, at peace with herself and her God.

Gone was her broken heart, the scent of her despair, her smothering fear.

Gone was the presence of Satan and his control of her life.

Mary's Search

 Mary Magdalene is not the wickedest woman in the Bible record. Absolutely not! The sin for which she was despised is not even listed among the seven things God hates most (Proverbs 6:17-19).

Her story reveals the same pain, fear, loss, degradation, hopelessness, and sorrow that women everywhere experience to one degree or another, at one time or another. But most of all, in her story the character of the Heart Mender is revealed, presenting a spectacle brilliant with unconditional love and sparkling with hope. Her story reminds us all of our need for healing and for a sense of value and purpose. Her experience confirms the existence of a Healer and teaches what every woman needs to know about her God.

The Bible records nothing of Mary's girlhood, but we can imagine her bent over a wildflower that has burst into unexpected bloom beside the dusty street. Hear her laugh at the antics of a lamb, and feel the roughness of the road beneath her bare feet as she hurries off to the marketplace.

We can guess at her thoughts as she sweeps the dust from the earthen floor of the little home she shares with Martha and Lazarus, dreaming of the moment she will care for her own home and sit at the table with her husband and children. How vulnerable she must be, a girl about to burst into womanhood. Ponder the dreams her heart must contain.

Then one day Satan, using one who promised love, snatched all her dreams away. The Bible does not tell how Simon convinced her to give herself to him, but the record shows that he took without giving the love and security her heart craved. We can only wonder at the lies, the broken promises and pain that followed.

In the end he came to despise her as a sinner, unmindful of his own sin against her, condemning her, as did most of her friends.

Drenched in fear and pressed down by guilt, Mary made more wrong choices, moving her further from her dreams and closer to despair. Soon her heart that had been created to hold love lay empty and broken. Her hopes turned to heaviness, her dreams to drudgery, her love to loathing. Others judged her without mercy and discarded her as trash. When she slipped into despair, Satan, who had plotted her ruin, came to control her life.

Then one morning Mary found herself thrown like a heap of rags at the feet of another Man. She dared not lift her eyes, but wept as she awaited his expected command: "Stone her!" After all, she deserved to die. She had broken the Commandment. She steeled herself against the crushing blow of the first rock, wondering how long it would take to die. A groan of agony pushed up from deep within her.

All she had ever wanted was to be loved.

These Women Searched Too

Shade your eyes from the noonday sun and look down a narrow

trail that leads from a small cluster of white houses to a well, protected by a mound of rocks. Catch the scuffle of footsteps, and watch a nameless woman draw near.

She is alone.

She has come to the well in the heat of the day to avoid the condemning glances of those who might know of her immoral lifestyle. Her heart is as empty as her water pot. She will easily fill it and drink of the cool water, but she understands nothing about One who can quench the deep thirst of her heart.

The funeral train winds its way through Nain. The sounds of a mother's sobs and the cries of those who walk with her fill the air. She trudges along the dusty road, following the body of her only son, who is draped over a narrow stretcher and is being born to a lonely grave. The loss of her child's love and companionship claws at her heart. Fear stomps its way across her mind.

"How will I support myself?" she cries, clinging to a friend. "Where will I live? I belong to no one. I will be forced to beg for a living for my son was the last male member of my family, and he has perished."

The surging mass of people press about Jesus, straining to catch His every word, to plead for His help. They pause now and again to witness another miracle of mercy. A woman shuffles along behind the crowd. She has long searched for relief, spilling out her woes into the ears of an endless stream of doctors, trying dozens of cures.

Now she searches for the One called Jesus.

Inside the doorway of a small house, perched on a rocky hillside, a widow, dressed in worn, unbleached garments, hunches over a clay bowl on a wooden table. She stirs flour, oil, and a little salt together. A small boy sits nearby, poking at a flickering fire his mother has built inside a small earthen oven.

This widow and her son do not hear the footsteps of a weary man, nor do they see him draw near their door. They see only the empty flour sack slumped against the wall. They hear only the cry of their own hearts, knowing that hunger will soon return—and then death.

Into a garden, lovely beyond description, steps the most breathtaking of all God's creation. She pauses by the forbidden tree when she hears a voice from a most unlikely source.

"Come close!" the serpent invites.

Eve is startled, but instead of fleeing to Adam's side she pauses as the serpent continues.

"Didn't God restrict your freedom by not allowing you to eat from any tree you wish?"

"No; no!" she protests. "God does not restrict our freedom. We may eat of any tree in the garden—except this one, here in the middle. God has asked us not to eat of it—or even to touch it—or we will die, for sure."

As she spoke, the woman could see how good the fruit looked as the serpent ate it.

And the evil one smiled. He knew of Eve's desires and dreams. Carefully he drew her into his trap, promising a new and expanded life.

She saw the fruit—it looked so good.

She heard the crunch as the serpent bit into a piece.

She could almost taste the sweet juice that dripped into shimmering pools on a leaf nearby. She smelled its sweetness, and desire awakened within her. "The fruit is safe," she reasoned, watching the serpent curl around the branch.

"God is a liar," the evil one whispered. "Nothing will happen to you if you disobey Him. He has not really provided for all your needs. God is selfish; He is keeping the best for Himself—He wants to keep you in ignorance. You are smart enough to choose for yourself." The voice paused, and a forked tongue flicked out to capture a droplet of the nectar. "God doesn't want you to be like Him. There is a lot more good stuff out there"—the serpent made a sweeping motion with his tail—"and you aren't going to get it from God. I can give it to you."

Eve wanted that fruit and all that it promised to give her. "God must be wrong," she decided.

So she took the fruit.

And she ate.

After only a bite she felt a surge of energy and power, just as the serpent had promised. Excited, she filled her arms full of the golden deliciousness and ran to find her husband.

And paradise was lost.

When she heard God's voice in the garden, she felt no joy, no expectation. She hid, fear's icy fingers clutching at her throat. Satan rejoiced as He watched Eve run away from the only One who could help her. Satan hoped it would be forever.

My Desperate Search for Love

Sirens screeched in the silent night, and blasts of red and blue light pierced the darkness. I bolted from my bed and ran to the window. Two cars sat in the driveway, lights flashing. Suddenly my bedroom door burst open and crashed against the wall. A man stood in the doorway. He looked around the room then spotted me at the window. He grabbed me in powerful arms and headed for the door. A terrible scream rose in my throat but couldn't escape. I heard my sister's door open. She yelled. Soon other screams filled the house.

The man carried me to one of the cars, opened the door, and shoved me roughly inside. I fell against my younger brother, who was hunched up on the car seat, whimpering. Then the man jumped into the front seat and started the car. As we sped away, I knelt on the seat and peered out the back window. The second car was following. I could see my older sister and three of my brothers clumped together in the back seat. They stared back at me with wide eyes.

The cars came to a stop in front of a building that stretched far out into the darkness. Small, barred windows dotted the walls.

I gasped.

The man jumped out, opened my door, and snatched me from the seat. He dragged me through a metal door into a huge room. I spotted my four brothers and two sisters and ran to them. We clung to each other, not speaking. I stared at four men who stood nearby, talking together.

"We got them all," said a man who was dressed in a police uniform.

"They were abandoned, all right," another added. "There wasn't a bit of food in the house, and the electricity had been turned off."

A door on the far wall opened, admitting a man who carried a huge wad of keys. He wore a khaki uniform and black boots. "You there," he said, pointing to my oldest brother, Glenn. And you two," he said, looking at Lynn and Bod, "come with me."

When they just stood, staring, he grabbed them by the shoulders and pushed them through the door.

"Where are you taking my brothers?" I screamed, running after them.

A hand reached out and dragged me back from the doorway.

Then another door opened, and a large woman in the same kind of khaki uniform entered. She towered above me, looking at me through dark, close-set eyes that bookended a hawk nose. She pinched her lips into a thin line and pushed a stray lock of hair into the clip that held her hair in a bun at the back of her head. She picked up my younger sister, Alice, and snarled, "I'm Iona. Come with me."

I wanted to run from that terrible woman, but I followed meekly. Only my mind found the courage to scream.

Iona led us down a long hall that was lined with doors and barred windows. Metal taps on the bottom of her boots clicked a staccato beat on the gray tiles. She stopped, opened one of the doors, and pushed us inside. "Go to sleep," she ordered. "I will come back in the morning."

My oldest sister, Anita, untied our shoes and told us to climb into the single bed on the right side of the room. Alice and Grover fell asleep immediately, but I lay silent, staring into the darkness. Anita got into a bed on the far side of the room. We did not speak.

After long moments I thought I heard muffled cries. "Are you all right?" I asked. My sister didn't answer. After a long time the sobbing stopped.

I awoke just as a narrow band of light was forming on the horizon. The door opened, and Iona's form completely filled the doorway. "Come with me," she ordered, glowering down at us.

I awakened my little brother and sister and pulled them out of bed. Two other women appeared at the door. They snatched Alice and Grover up, then Iona led me away. I did not see where Anita went.

Iona took me to a large shower room where she stripped me and pushed me into the running water. I couldn't move. The warm water flowed over me until Iona pulled me away. She wrapped me in a towel and took me to a large room where more than 20 cots lined the walls. She sat me on a cot near the end of one of the rows.

"This is yours. Put your things into this cabinet," she said, pointing to a tall, metal cupboard that stood beside the bed.

"I have no things," I whispered. They had taken everything, even my clothes. There was nothing familiar to comfort me—not a book or a toy, or even a piece of clothing. Tears threatened to spill over, but I couldn't cry.

Girls sitting on nearby cots turned to stare at me. Their eyes looked round and dull, and their shoulders drooped. No one spoke.

"Go to that open door and get into line," Iona said, leading me from the cot.

I stood there, naked, frightened, and ashamed. Six other girls stood in front of me, staring at the floor. When my turn came a woman, who was standing in the doorway, spoke to me. "Do you know your size?" she asked.

I couldn't speak.

"You look like an eight," she decided, hardly glancing at me. Then she turned, snatching shoes, socks, underwear, and a dress from the rows of shelves that clung to the walls. "Put these on," she said.

I took the stack of clothes to my cot and put them on. The shoes were too big; my feet slid around inside them. The faded dress felt stiff, but I put it on. Then I stared at myself. I didn't look like me at all. I was afraid I had become totally lost. I flung myself onto the bed and sobbed. "Where am I? What is this place? Why am I here?"

No one answered me.

"You better come," a thin voice said, after a while. "They'll get pretty mad if you're late."

I wiped my eyes and looked up.

"My name's Marty. I'm 10," the girl said. She looked as thin as her voice. She smiled weakly and walked away. I followed her. We entered a room filled with tables. Children of all ages stood in line, holding empty metal trays.

I followed the girls who were getting into line. When I reached the head of the line I handed my tray to a woman as I had seen others do. The women ladled eggs and cereal onto the tray. She added a piece of toast and smeared on a slab of butter. I followed Marty to a table. She picked at her food, but I couldn't eat at all. I laid my head down on the table and put my hands in my lap

Suddenly Iona reappeared. "Time for school," she said.

The girls jumped up and trailed after her. I had to follow, too, though I felt weak and could hardly keep up with the group. We walked down a long concrete sidewalk and past neat, brick houses. Children stopped playing to stare at us. After what seemed like forever, we stopped at a chain-link fence. Iona opened a gate, and we entered a schoolyard. Children lined the fence, staring at us.

"Look!" a boy yelled. "The Juvie kids are here." They all broke out in laughter and made faces at us.

"Murderers!" a girl screamed. "Look at the murderers!"

"What's a Juvie kid?" I asked Marty, who stood beside me. "Why did they call us murderers?"

"Don't you know?" she said. "We live at Juvenile Hall."

"Why did they call us murderers," I asked again, staring wide-eyed at the children.

"Oh, they're right. I really did murder my father," Marty said matter-of-factly, looking at me with dull eyes. "I hated him," she said simply, her eyes looking into some faraway place.

"But you're only 10!" I said, staring at her.

She didn't answer.

Iona led me to a classroom and pushed me into a desk near the door. I didn't see or hear anything else that happened that day. I didn't know when I was led home at the end of the day.

Marty, the murderer, slept two cots down from mine. I stared at her long after she fell asleep. The muscles in her face twitched, and she thrashed about in the bed. Could it be true that Marty had killed her father and the police had brought her to this place called Juvenile Hall? But why was I here? I hadn't done anything bad. The policeman had said I was abandoned.

For 11 months I stood in line to receive someone else's castoff clothing, to eat food I hadn't selected, and to go to a school I hated. The hopelessness, the pain, and the fear seeped deep into my soul.

Although I didn't know it, I had begun a search for love. For security. For a reason to live.

Modern Eves Still Search

Today we still search—wounded, weary, frightened, sin-sick, and hungry. We search for a sense of meaning, a way to belong, for comfort, love, and joy. We want answers to our questions. Why am I here, and where am I going? We want to know if there is anything or anyone at the end of broken dreams. Like our sisters in ancient times, we experience the effects of sin in our world. We have been abused, misused, rejected, ignored, and have seen our dreams dashed to pieces. If you think this is too bleak a picture, just look at the reality of the pain in your own heart and in the lives of other women around you.

But there is good news. Jesus, the Heart Mender, knows your struggle. He knows what events shaped your heart and wounded you. He knows that it's His love you need, His acceptance and help. He waits for you to weary of useless searching for these things apart from Him. He draws near through nature, through His word and the love of others, wanting you to see Him and call out for help. Sometimes He even groans in longing.

> "'Be appalled, O heavens, at this,
> And shudder, be very desolate,'" declares the Lord.
> "'For My people have committed two evils:
> They have forsaken Me,
> The fountain of living waters,

> To hew for themselves cisterns,
> Broken cisterns,
> That can hold no water.'"
> "Seek the Lord while He may be found;
> Call upon Him while He is near."
> —Jeremiah 2:12, 13; Isaiah 55:6 (NASB)

Can you hear His heart cry in these words? Listen to the agony in His voice as He calls upon the inhabitants of heaven to shudder at our pain and the methods we choose to bring love and security to our lives. He stands horrified because you and I forsake Him. We turn away, looking for love and answers apart from Him. "All we like sheep have gone astray" (Isa. 53:6). All have wandered from the fountain of cool water, from the safety of the sheepfold, from the loving care of the Shepherd. We have searched for better water, greener grass, and safer shelter.

God isn't appalled that we feel our need, or that we search. He understands this; He invites it. He is amazed and grieved that we search apart from Him. And this search apart from Him has brought us bitter water, blighted grasses, and leaky shelters. His grief is that we "dig our own wells," that we try to solve our own problems and meet our own needs, choosing our own methods.

Eve did this. She chose Satan's plan over God's because it seemed the best way to accomplish her desires.

Satan, the liar, entices us to think God is keeping something good from us, or that He has abandoned us altogether. He urges us to sample the things he claims will expand our happiness. He smacks his evil lips with satisfaction when we choose his way and suffer the results of our wrong choices, or the wrong choices of others. Hurt and disillusioned, we go on searching. We weary in our search, for now we carry a load of guilt.

The Heart Mender Is Calling Your Name

We have a choice to make. We will hear the voice of Satan, just as Eve did, for he still sneaks into our gardens. He will tell us that God is not the answer to our problems, that He is a liar and does not

25

care for us. He will suggest that we have made too big a mess of our lives, that our situation is hopeless. He will parade our faults before us until we cry out in horror. Then he will offer solutions that numb the pain but separate us from God, causing us the greatest pain of all. If we choose to listen and act on his suggestions, he will plunge us deeper into despair, as He did Mary Magdalene.

But wait! The Heart Mender is in the garden, too. He knows our story. He understands our search. The one who is everlasting in mercy and full of forgiveness positions Himself where we will find Him. There are truths about Him that every woman needs to know.

Listen!

The Heart Mender is calling your name. "Choose to trust me," He cries. "Don't give in to panic. Your case is not hopeless—I can do anything. Resist the temptation to figure everything out by yourself. Just cry, "Help!"

Choose!

Give the Heart Mender full control of your life. Listen only to Him. Ignore the stares. Keep your eyes on His face.

When Mary lifted her head from the dust of the street, she saw Jesus and discovered a forgiveness brilliant with life-changing power.

The woman at the well listened, believed, and accepted the love that quenched her thirst and ended her search.

The weeping widow, whose hopes lay as dead as the son she mourned, met the Resurrection and the Life. At His words, her son leaped into her life again.

The nameless woman who searched for health touched the Great Physician and years of suffering ended.

And a hungry woman and her son ate manna from heaven.

Listen to the voice of the Heart Mender:

"This is what the Lord says,
    the One who created you,
    the One who made you. . . .
    'Don't be afraid. I have redeemed you.
    I have named you. You are mine!'"
                —Isaiah 43:1

He alone can end your search and help you discover love.

The Heart Mender knows your struggle.
He knows that it's His love you need.

CHAPTER TWO

The Discovery

God doesn't always save us from heartache,
but He can keep us from despair.

MARY'S DISCOVERY

They sit on the cool tiles of the Temple floor, hundreds of them, listening to the One called Jesus. His words awaken hope in their hearts and shine like beams of light into their souls, the awareness of His love opening like a rosebud to the kiss of the morning sunlight.

But suddenly the peace is shattered. A dozen priests and Pharisees push their way through the crowd, dragging a resisting, weeping woman whom they throw at Jesus' feet. She doesn't look up, but lies there, sobbing.

"Master!" they shout. "This woman was caught in the act of committing adultery. What should we do with her? Moses told us that such a person should be stoned to death. What do You say?"

Every eye fastens on the terrified woman as the words of the Pharisees stab the stillness. Some of the faces in the crowd reflect the Pharisees' sneer; others reveal a shuddering horror.

The Pharisees step closer to Jesus, hatred burning in their eyes. They stand with arms folded over their chests, jaws set firm, faces devoid of any pity for the woman whose plight they've made as public as possible.

Every eye shifts from the woman and her tormenters to Him. What will He say? How will He treat this woman? His whole being is so transparent with feeling that they can almost read His thoughts in each new expression that flickers across his face. Is that sorrow? Yes. His heart is grieved by the cruelty of these men, smug in their self-righteousness. Yet they can see that He does not hate them— His eyes fill with longing. He wants to reach inside their hard hearts with His love.

Then He looks at the woman, His eyes gentle, a slight smile forming on his lips. Deep compassion flows from Him like springs of living water.

The religious leaders press forward. They point at the woman, leering, unmindful that they have broken the law themselves in bringing the woman before Jesus in this manner. Only her husband has that right.

But this is not about the woman; it is about hatred of Jesus. They have set a trap for Him.

And everyone knows it. A dozen solutions dart through their minds, but they know none of them will deliver this woman nor extricate Jesus.

Time stands still.

Jesus gazes for a moment at the proud religious leaders. He does not step back. He doesn't argue. He doesn't ridicule the woman nor heap more shame upon her. Instead, He writes, stooping down and tracing words in the dust on the tiles of the Temple floor.

When Jesus looks up He says, "'Any one of you who has never sinned, let him throw the first stone'" (John 8:7).

The woman cringes, bracing herself against the crushing blow of the first rock.

The silence echoes against the stone walls.

Jesus leans forward and starts writing again. This time the leaders push closer to better decipher the dusty characters. As quickly as they read, they slink away, one by one, confronted by not only their own secret sins but their part in trapping the woman

Soon only a small crowd remains with Jesus and the woman. All are silent.

Then Jesus stands again and speaks. "Mary, where are all those who were accusing you? It looks as though they've gone. There's no one here to condemn you." He reaches out and grasps her hand, lifting her to her feet, and wipes the tears from her cheeks.

For the first time Mary lifts her eyes and looks into His face, seeing what the crowd has seen, knowing that she sees there could change her life. Her eyes fill with wonder.

"You're right, Lord. There's not one," she answers, timidly looking about her at the silent crowd.

"'Neither will I condemn you,'" Jesus says, laying His hand upon her shoulder. "'I've forgiven you. So you may go, but leave your life of sin.'" He takes her hand and lifts her to her feet.

Unspeakable joy floods her heart. Moments before she had faced certain death, flung like a dirty rag onto the ground. But now she stands, head held high and face aglow. She is loved, and she knows it. She is forgiven, and she feels free. She takes her first tentative steps into a new life. "Surely this is the Son of God," someone whispers.

Jesus motions to those who stand in stunned silence to come close. The tricksters, the finger pointers, and the ones who condemn have gone. Delight dances in His eyes. "I am the Light of the World," He says. He smiles at Mary, His radiant love reaching out to include all who gaze at His face.

They move closer.

How I Discovered Love

Eleven months passed slowly. I wore someone else's clothes, ate food someone chose for me, and obeyed commands made by people who did not love me. I slept beside troubled children who had committed terrible crimes, who screamed in the night, and stared through vacant eyes. No one explained anything to me. No one bothered to comfort me. I had no idea when I would ever leave Juvenile Hall, where my parents had gone, nor what my brothers and sisters were doing. I caught fleeting glimpses of them in dark hallways and heard their distant voices over fences. Once I clung to them through a chain link fence, but adults pried us apart. I learned well the lessons of insecurity, fear, and loneliness.

One morning I found a worn book in the bottom of my locker. Bible, it said on the front. I had been taught that God created the world and that the Bible was His book. I realized, as I picked up the book, that I had not thought of God for a long time. I flipped the pages, passing books called Isaiah, Jeremiah, and Ezekiel. I felt a surge of longing to discover what the Book had to say, but I couldn't concentrate on the words. I flung the book back into the bottom of my locker. Certainly God had abandoned me just as my father had.

My usually happy self died under the strain of these negative emotions, and I fell ill. I awoke one morning hardly able to breathe. When I did not come to the line for clothing, Iona looked for me. She found me lying in my bed, gasping for air. She grabbed me, running down the hall, her boots thumping on the floor. "Call an ambulance!" I heard her cry to another woman. "She's real sick."

The ambulance arrived, but I hardly noticed. It took all my energy to suck a small bit of air into my lungs and even more to push it out again. I felt like a limp dishrag. I couldn't speak or resist whatever anyone wanted to do to me.

In the hospital doctors and nurses placed me in an oxygen tent, jabbed me with needles, and listened to my lungs. I continued to struggle for every breath. Then, after two days, I just gave up. I couldn't try anymore. Why should I? I didn't belong to anyone. I was alone. Abandoned. I thought about the girl I used to be—alive, optimistic, and always laughing. That girl had died. She was gone. There was nothing left to identify myself as her. Now I couldn't even breathe. I might as well just go to sleep.

I closed my eyes. I didn't struggle to take in another breath for a long time. I felt strangely at peace. When I opened my eyes for a moment, I saw a young doctor staring at me through the open door of my hospital room. Suddenly he reached into his pocket and pulled out a pen knife. He started to run toward me. He opened the knife and the blade flashed in the light from the window. When he jammed the blade into my throat, I didn't care. I didn't have enough air in my lungs to enable me to care. Nor did I respond to the burst of pain that swept over me. I didn't feel like I was even in myself anymore.

Suddenly a great ball of mucous shot through the hole he had

31

carved in my throat. I saw it hit him in the forehead. He wiped his head and stood looking at me. Then he grabbed me by the shoulders and shook me. I felt a tremendous release of pressure, then involuntarily sucked in air. Great drafts of sweet air filled my lungs. I coughed and breathed in more air. Then I fell into darkness as I felt myself being lifted to a gurney and rolled down the hall in great haste.

When I awoke, I lay on a bed beside a giant machine that wheezed and clattered as it pushed air in and out of my lungs through a long tube. Nurses came and went. They sat at a desk by the head of my bed where I couldn't see them. I felt completely alone. They bathed me, suctioned my lungs, and changed my I.V. bottle, but they did not speak. It was as though they didn't want to know me. After all, I was only going to die. I followed them with my eyes, the only part of my body that could move.

One day a new nurse entered the room. She smiled. Then she spoke to me. "Hello! My name is Miss Laura. I'll be taking care of you today."

All I could do was stare, but I felt a sense of pleasure at her presence. Each time she suctioned me, turned me, or gave me a treatment, she explained what she was doing. She spoke to me as if I were a real person, a person who might live again.

Then one day she set up a mirror over the head of my bed. She turned it at an angle so that I could look into it and see her sitting at the desk. I watched as she wrote in the chart and did other paper work. Sometimes she looked up at me and smiled. My world had expanded a bit.

Another day she arrived carrying a black book. She laid it on the desk. After making me comfortable, she sat down and opened the book. *What is she reading?* I wondered. I looked into her face. It looked happy. I stared at her for a long time until a sudden spasm of coughing grabbed me. She jumped up and ran to my side. She held me up and gently applied the suction to my lungs. Her arms felt good around me. When I calmed down, she laid me back down and busied herself around the room.

I rested, feeling more comfortable than usual. My eyes caught the open book in the mirror. I could just make out the title on the upper left margin. Since the letters were upside down, it took me a while to make out the word, but finally I read Jeremiah 29. I struggled to read more, and gradually I made out the message on the page:

"I already know the plans I have for you. I will help you, not hurt you. I will give you a future and a hope. You will call on me and I will answer. You will talk to me and I will listen. You will search me and find me as you search for me with all your heart" (verses 11-13).

The strain of reading the message in the book exhausted me, but the words brought a change in my thinking. I let them pass through my mind hour after hour, day after day. I knew that the "I" in the verses must be God. He had plans for me. He wanted to help me, give me a future and hope. I felt convinced that in spite of my situation I could call on Him and receive some kind of help. The God that promised these things must love me. He understood my situation—I couldn't even breath on my own. Yet He clearly said that He knew His plans for me.

Plans. A future.

Help. Hope.

Searching.

Listening.

The words, like living seeds planted in the receptive soil of my heart, took root. Although the journey would be long, I had turned a corner, begun a searching, started connecting. I had discovered love.

A month later my parents secured our dismissal from Juvenile Hall. We went to live in the mountains of Southern California. Among the great trees, the laughing brooks, and the nodding wild flowers, I discovered the God who loved me. I awaited His plans with eagerness.

The real miracle is God's covering, His protection in the worst of circumstances.

These, too, God Touched with His Love

Childless Sarah, too old to conceive, laughs when God promises she will bear a child. "Nine months from now," He tells Abraham, "I'll be back, after your wife Sarah gives birth to a son" (See Genesis 18:10).

Hope, once bold and alive, has died inside her. But the next time she laughs, it bursts from a heart delighted by fulfilled promise. She holds a long-awaited child in her arms. Hope becomes reality, and Sarah discovers that the One who loves her can do anything.

He keeps His promises.

Noah's wife lives in a world in which people push thoughts of God far away. She watches sin take hold of her world and deepen and spread like a cancer. Although surrounded by those who make evil practices a way of life, she teaches her children to know and obey God. Then one day God speaks to Noah, informing him of the coming deluge. She looks into the face of her children and feels fear. However, with the news of impending loss comes the assurance that a way of escape has been provided by a God who loves her.

When Noah comes home with news of a great rescue plan, given to him by God, she encourages him to obey and build the ark. As Noah preaches the messages sent him from God, she listens. She watches her sons add plank after plank to the huge skeleton that is destined to be a lifeboat, grasping the promise of rescue close to her heart. She has come to trust the words of the One who loves her, and all those He has created.

As she walks into the ark behind her sons and their wives, while others all around her have chosen rebellion and cling to their fear, she discovers saving love.

Rebecca stands in the door of a tent. A hot wind blows her robe and lifts a strand of the girl's long hair, setting it dancing. She sighs. She is dreaming of her future: Who will my father choose as a husband for me? Whenever male guests arrive, she steals a peek at them through the tent flap and listens to their conversations. She wonders,

Will my father find a man who is kind, and who will love me?

Rebecca thinks of Sarah. Everyone knows that her husband, Abraham, is a good man.

Not only that, but God worked a miracle to give them a child. Would God choose for her? Did He care about her future? Would He help her father find someone she could love?

Then Eleazar came across the desert with camels and gifts. He told the story of Abraham, and of a son who needed a wife. He said that God had chosen her to be that woman.

Rebecca recognized God's loving intervention in the arrangement. She said, "I will go and become Isaac's wife."

She left her family and journeyed into a faraway land.

She discovered love in the heart of a God who cared.

What an Angel Wing Taught Me About God's Love

"Get in!" my friend Martha commanded, opening the car door. "I'm taking you to the beach. You need a few days to kick sand and bask in the sunshine. I know you're fighting discouragement. Your future must seem so uncertain. Divorce is awful."

I slumped into the front seat. The Demon Fear jumped in beside me. I tried to push negative thoughts away while I waited for Martha to pack our bags into the trunk.

I feel so unloved! I wailed silently to God, *Help my belief in Your care for me chase away these nagging fears about my future before they smother me with discouragement.*

At the sight of the palm trees swaying on Florida's border, I felt some excitement creeping into my numb mind. We drove down the full length of Sanibel and stopped at a cottage that sat on the bay side of the island. The sandy beaches lay just across the narrow arm of land, and we could see both the bay and the beach from our windows.

"Let's get out there and find shells," Martha said when we had unpacked our things. "I know this trip to the beach can't solve your problems, but it will help heal your heart."

"I hope you're right," I sighed, wanting to believe it could happen. "I think I'll go for a walk." I needed some time alone.

"Go on," Martha urged. "I'll come along in a few minutes.

The screen door slammed behind me as I headed for the bay side of the island where hundreds of acres of mud flats lay exposed by the receding tide. I gazed out over a narrow waterway that separated me from the flats. *Everything out there is covered with slimy, brown mud. That's the way I feel: covered by the slime of discouragement,* I thought.

A small motorboat sped by. It made its way along the edge of the muddy land, then stopped. An elderly couple threw over an anchor, climbed out, and sloshed their way over the mud. Soon the woman's voice rang out: "Look at this, Charles!"

Her husband tried to rush to her side through the thick mud. I laughed in spite of myself when his right leg sank into the mud past his knee. He grabbed the entrapped member with both hands and yanked it from the mud and plunged on. This time he was able to stand up, and only his ankles sank out of sight. Finally, he stood beside the woman, who dropped to her knees and began to dig a large hole in the mud.

I couldn't believe my eyes when most of her arm disappeared into the slimy pit. Then she suddenly stood up, bringing half the mud in the flats with her. She held a large blob of mud in her hands, lifting it toward the sun like a rare gem. They both stared and smiled.

"Linda, I believe that's your best specimen ever!" he declared, smiling into her face.

Linda placed the muddy object in a plastic box and closed the lid with great care. She pushed back her floppy hat, leaving a muddy smudge on her forehead, and headed off across the flats.

I watched her stop from time to time and poke her fingers into the mud and felt a longing to discover the treasure that made them laugh with such delight. But when I looked at the murky river of water that separated me from the couple, I shook my head. Then, with a burst of determination, I plunged in.

"What are you doing?" Martha cried with alarm when she arrived at the water's edge.

"I'm going over there," I said, pointing toward the mud-spattered couple.

"Come back!" Martha screamed. "There might be sting rays in that water—or something worse. You can't see the bottom!"

"No," I called over my shoulder. "I have to see the treasure!"

It felt creepy, sliding my feet along the gooey bottom. I wanted to swim, but a swift current of water flowed toward the sea. I knew that if I lifted both feet off the bottom at once I would be swept away, so I just plunged ahead, keeping my eyes on Linda's face, drawn on by her laughter. Halfway across, the water reached my waist, then my shoulders. Soon, only my head stuck out of the stream of brown water. Then my feet struck a steep bank, and I struggled up and out, onto the mud flats.

I turned and looked back. Martha had plunged into the current and stumbled after me. I smiled. *I survived it, so she's coming, too,* I thought. "You can do it!" I called to her. I waited until she reached me, then we both slogged through the mud toward the couple.

"Don't leave your foot in one place too long," I warned Martha. "It's really sticky." When we finally reached the couple, they were kneeling in muck, enlarging a small hole.

"What are you looking for?" I asked, peering into the bucket full of muddy objects.

"Oh, hello," they both said, looking up.

"Angel wings," Charles said.

"We're having a great time," Linda added. Her eyes danced with delight. "Treasure is where you least expect it." She bent over the mud hole again.

It didn't look like fun. It looked awful. I couldn't see anything but mud. But I had to admit that these people had my curiosity at full alert.

"How do I find an angel wing?" I asked.

"Just look for a small hole," Linda said, sweeping her hands over the flats. "Stick your finger down into it. If it goes straight down, you've located the burrow of an angel wing."

"OK," I said, and started my search for a perfect hole.

I hadn't gone far when I spotted one. I stooped and stuck my finger into it. My finger plunged down a few inches, then the hole veered off to the right.

"If your finger goes off to one side, draw it out quickly," Charles instructed. "Those are crab holes."

I yanked my finger out of the hole and jumped to my feet. "You didn't say anything about crabs," I complained.

He just shrugged.

I plodded around in the mud for 10 minutes before finding another hole. I hesitated a moment, then stuck my finger in about two inches. The hole veered off to one side. "Oh!" I screamed, pulling my finger out faster than a bolt of lightning strikes.

"I guess that was a crab hole," Charles observed dryly. "Don't give up," he added.

After trying four holes, I found one that felt smooth and round and plunged straight down. "I've got one!" I yelled.

Charles struggled over. He showed me how to dig the mud away from the hard narrow burrow. "Keep digging until your hands can get beneath the shell, then lift it out."

I stooped down and grabbed a clump of mud from one side of the hole. Linda and Martha sloshed over to watch.

"This could take a long time," I warned as I removed another lump of mud.

"Keep digging," Linda said.

I dug around and around the narrow hole, turning it into a large pit. Every time I removed mud from the hole, I had to plunge my arm deeper to get the next fist full.

"Get on your knees," Martha instructed.

So I did what I had to do: I knelt down and dug. Soon the hole swallowed up my entire arm, so I just stretched out on my stomach, down in the mud, and dug some more.

"I'm sure you'll touch the shell soon," Linda encouraged.

I decided to speed things up. I grabbed a big glob of mud.

"Look out for the—" Linda started to say.

A sharp pain shot through my fingers. "It bit me!" I screamed, yanking my hand from the hole. Blood and mud ran down my three middle fingers.

"I guess you found it," Charles said.

Linda shook her head. "Let me see your fingers. It didn't bite you—you slashed your fingers over the sharp tip of the shell." She pulled three large, very soiled adhesive bandages from a pocket, wrapping one around each finger. The nurse in me cringed.

"Better give her a glove," Charles said.

She grabbed a mud-saturated garden glove from her pocket that had dried in a grotesque position. Undeterred, she banged it against her leg, then jammed it over my hand and tied it around my wrist with a shoe lace.

"You're in too big a hurry," she said, pushing back her floppy hat and leaving another blob of mud behind. "The edges of the angel wing are sharp. You've reached the top of the shell. Dig around it another six inches, then lift it out."

I looked at my gloved hand and shook my head. My fingers throbbed. "Oh, well," I sighed, flinging myself onto the mud and poking my arm back into the hole I had made. "I hope the shell is worth it. How can it survive in such a terrible place, covered with a blanket of mud?"

"The angel wing burrows into the mud—its home," Linda explained. "Sometimes it digs as deep as 18 inches, but it can stretch two siphon tubes up to the surface. When the tide brings in food and fresh water, the angel wing sucks it in. Although it lives in the mud, it is not muddy itself. Look, the shell is covered by a thin, transparent skin that actually separates it from the mud."

Only after mud covered my arm, clung to my hair, and dripped from my chin did I reach the bottom of the angel wing. I wiggled it back and forth, gently lifting it to the surface.

Linda snatched it from my hand, dipped it into a small pool of water nearby, and gently rubbed the mud away. She peeled back a thin skin, and we all stared at the delicate white shell, decorated with fine sculptured lines.

Then Martha dug her own angel wing shell, and Charles and Linda ferried us across the now-swollen waterway and deposited us on the shore near our cottage. People stared, but we just smiled and clung to our treasures.

"Don't forget to soak them in a little bleach," Linda called after us. "It will remove the remainder of the covering."

"Thank you!" we said, waving to them as we headed for the cottage.

We ran to the kitchen and placed our treasures in the sink. We rinsed the angel wings, then removed the mollusk creature and placed the shells in a bowl of 100-percent bleach. A few minutes later we lifted them from the bleach with tongs and laid them on paper towels. All trace of the mud was gone. Each shell looked perfect, clean, and white, like the wings of an angel.

I suddenly realized that God had used this adventure to teach me a lesson and paint a picture of Himself on my heart.

"This whole experience is like my life, Martha," I told her as we stared at the shells. "I was going along pretty good until I fell into the mud flats of discouragement."

"You had a reason," Martha said loyally. "You looked for love—and found divorce. That's a tragedy."

"True," I agreed. "But discouragement is an option. I've been bogged down in it."

"God doesn't always choose to save us from heartaches, but He can keep us from despair," Martha said, giving me a meaningful glance.

I remembered the effort, excitement, and the joy I had just experienced in discovering and digging out the beautiful shell. "The lesson of the angel wing is very clear," I said, staring down at the white shells. "He sees me as a special treasure, no matter how anyone else views me. He knows I am lost in the mud, and He wants to rescue me."

"It cost Him more than a bandaged finger," Martha said, pointing to my bandaged hand. "It cost Him His life. But I bet He just loves to rescue people," she added

I dropped into a chair. *You know where I am, God. Please dig me out.* "Once He finds us, do you think that He carries us as carefully as we did those angel wings," I asked Martha.

"Yes, I do. I also think He is fully able to get the mud off without breaking us."

We waited until the angel wing shells were dry, then wrote the number "1" one on each specimen and placed that number in a special notebook. Beside the number, we added the name of the shells and described the location where we found them. Now they belonged to our special collection.

> *The lesson of the angel wing is clear.*
> *God sees you as a special treasure,*
> *no matter how you're viewed by others.*

The Real Miracle

"Do you know what the real miracle is here?" I asked Martha. "It's the covering," I added, not waiting for her to answer. "The skin covers the shell. It is almost invisible, yet it perfectly encloses the treasure, keeping all the mud off. The dark mud would stain and ruin the shell, but the skin protects it. What the covering is to the shell, the invisible covering of God's love is to anyone who chooses Jesus."

The temptation to doubt this love and give in to the darkness of discouragement surrounded me, sticky and black like the mud in the flats. But I could choose to let Jesus wrap me in His love, in His own presence. He had found me, and now He held me in His hands. I belonged. I was treasure. No matter what else changed, that hadn't—and never would.

He didn't condemn me.

He wasn't throwing rocks.

He would wash away the dark sorrow in His own time and way.

But now—right now—I could be safe from the destructive power of discouragement and despair. Surely the One who provided all this loved me. I could trust Him for my future.

My search for love had ended.

At last.

You, too, Can Discover Love

What will you discover when your search ends at the feet of Jesus? What will you see when you look up into His face? Imagine it: the One who calls Himself the Water of Life is washing away your shame, your sorrow, and the marks left by others' hate. The God of heaven is pouring His healing love into your heart. You don't have to brace yourself for a lecture or steel yourself against thrown rocks or wagging fingers. No! You see acceptance radiating from His eyes, and it sets your heart free. It hushes every voice but His.

Reach out and grasp the thought that Jesus, who dares to say "I forgive you," *can*. The One who claims to be the Son of God, *is*. He who appears to love, *does*.

You and I didn't sit in the temple on that long ago morning, but when we read Mary's story, the scene etches itself into our hearts and minds. We haven't seen the face of Jesus as she did, but we can imagine it. We can enter into the same experience, because God sent Jesus in the flesh to make sure we would see unconditional love with our own eyes.

He's determined that we fully understand that His forgiveness and love covers all women at all times in all circumstances, whether caught in their own sin or in the results of the sin of other. He wants us to experience the soothing power of love poured over the deep wounds that Satan has carved into our hearts. Then He wants us to feast at the banquet of His love. To be surrounded by it, encased within it, protected by it.

Every woman can say:

"O Lord, you have searched my heart and know me inside and out. You are behind me, in front of me and all around me wherever I go. You have touched me and drawn me close to you.

"I can't comprehend [it]. It's so wonderful that no matter how hard I try to understand, I can't grasp it all. Where can I go to leave the presence of your Spirit? Where shall I run that you're not already there? If I were to launch out into space, you'd be there. If I were to tunnel into the depths of the earth, you'd be there. If I had wings and could fly to the ends of the earth or to the most remote island in the sea, your presence would be there and your arms would be ready to hold me" (Psalm 139:1, 5-10).

Our God knows.

He knows your circumstances, your sin, and the sins of others who have hurt you.

He feels your joy, your pain and fear.

He understands your longings and dreams.

In spite of all this knowledge, He wants you. He wants you before you even realize that you're lost, before you're out of the pit, before you're clean. He wants you! He longs to enclose you with His love, to hold you close to His heart.

Think about it. Savor the truth that God loves you like that.

Listen to the God who says, "I will personally go and search for my sheep and care for them. As a good shepherd watches over his sheep and takes care of them, so will I watch over my sheep and will take care of them. I will go and look for them and bring them back from wherever they've been scattered on a day of overhanging clouds and thick darkness. . . . I myself will be their shepherd and take care of them. I will have them come and lie down and be at peace" (Ezekiel 34:11-15).

Accepting love—forgiving love, healing love—that lasts forever is not a dream; it's a certainty. Open your Bible and watch Jesus comfort the sorrowful, lift up the discouraged, touch lepers, revive the dead, forgive the sinner, and laugh with children. Discover love as you have never seen it before.

When you discover His love, your pain and fear will subside.

When you discover love, you want to sit at His feet.

CHAPTER THREE

The Fight Against Fear

I decided not to hate and blame. I had to let go of these
so God could fill me with something better.

MARY'S GREATEST FEAR

"She's coming!" Martha said, grabbing Lazarus's arm. "Look! She's at the top of the hill. . . . O God, let her be truly free this time." She flung herself into her brother's arms and muffled her sobs in the sleeve of his robe.

Lazarus patted her gently. "I'm comforted by the fact that she always goes back to Jesus. Surely He has found a way to help her."

Martha leaned back so she could look at her brother's face. "Six times, Lazarus! Six times Jesus has cast out the demons that trouble her. And always she slips back into sin. It hurts me so."

"I know," Lazarus soothed. "It's because you love her so much. I love her, too. But we must trust Jesus. Remember, He heals lepers, gives sight to the blind, and opens the ears of the deaf. Surely He can free our Mary! We must have faith, Martha." He touched her face. "She is almost here. Wipe your tears."

Martha dabbed at her face with the edge of her garment and produced a weak smile.

When Mary spotted Lazarus and Martha standing in the doorway, she began to run down the hill. She waved her hands and called out: "Lazarus, Martha! I'm free. This time I'm really free!"

Martha and Lazarus glanced at each other, then, when Mary reached them, they opened their arms to her.

"Come; eat. I know you must be hungry." Martha moved Mary toward the door of their home.

"Oh, no!" Mary objected. "Not now. I want to talk with both of you. Let's sit here in the shade of the tree."

The three settled on the grass beneath the sycamore tree that cast its shade over the front door.

"I am free—free at last!" Mary exclaimed, her face shining. "But I know what you're thinking—"

"You don't have to explain anything," Lazarus interrupted. "We're just glad you're home."

"But I want to," Mary said, placing her hand on his shoulder. She looked at Martha. "Six times Jesus has prayed for me and set me free of the terrible demons. Each time I began a new life of obedience to God with hope in my heart. But fear always moved in . . . and grew until—"

"Fear?" Martha questioned. "Fear was your problem?"

"Yes. I was afraid that Jesus was not the Messiah as He claimed, that He hadn't really forgiven me, and that His power would not keep me free in the future. I was afraid you wouldn't want me here at home. I became discouraged, and then—well, you know what happened. But this time it's different!" she shouted, standing up to face them.

"Of course it is," Lazarus said.

"Please, Mary, tell us why. Why is it different?" Martha urged.

Mary sat down. A light came into her eyes they hadn't seen before. She smiled, but she didn't speak for a moment. "What I have experienced is beyond words," she began finally. "But I know this: the fear is gone. Gone! Don't you see? My fear was unbelief. It separated me from Him. That's why Satan returned. But for the past three weeks I've followed Jesus. I saw a crippled man leap to his feet at Jesus' command. My heart burst with joy when He opened the eyes of a blind child, and she reached up a small hand and touched the first face she had ever seen. His words found their way into my heart, and the fear evaporated like dew on the rose of Sharon in the garden. I know now that He is the Son of God. I know He has power to completely heal me. I realize that I must stay close to Jesus, listen to His words, allow my trust in Him to grow. I must— Oh, I almost left Him altogether!" Her voice caught, and tears ran down her cheeks.

"But you didn't," Martha said, pulling her sister close. "You didn't."

"Thank God!" Lazarus's strong arms encircled them both. "Thank God our Mary is home to stay."

My Fight With Fear

I wandered along Sanibel Island's shoreline, absorbed in my thoughts. I hardly noticed when the golden sun peeked over the horizon, then eased itself into the sky.

I thought about my life. God certainly had a plan for me. He had helped me through the nursing course at Pacific Union College. I had married and had three wonderful children. My husband had chosen the ministry, so I had all the adventures of that lifestyle—and had loved every minute of it.

But suddenly my life had changed. Within the past year one of my sons married and moved away and my daughter set out for college in a distant state. Then I received a notice from a Las Vegas court announcing that my husband had sought, and received, a divorce!

A divorce.

From me.

I was alone.

I felt abandoned, betrayed, and bewildered. My life felt like a ship, far from shore, snatched up by a raging sea and flung about by hurricane winds. In the darkness, I couldn't see any harbor lights nor find the charts. A thick fog of pain hid God from my view.

Almost as soon as news of our divorce reached people, women began to approach me and pour out their own stories. Perhaps they felt I could understand them now that I knew what real loss was all about. They told me about loneliness, work stress, entanglement with drugs, fears of all kinds, children's death, cancer, hate, betrayal, financial failure, rebellious children, abuse, and rejection.

Added to the overwhelming weight of my own pain was the knowledge of others' sorrows. Depression and panic threatened to engulf me as I struggled to hang onto the reality of a God who loved me. "Will you leave me, too?" my heart cried.

The Sting Ray

As I walked along the beach, considering these things, I noticed the faint pattern of a small sting ray in the sand ahead. The ray's dagger tail thrashed back and forth in the air, and its "wings" beat against the beach like a pelican trying to fly up from the water. I knew the ray would die unless it reached water soon, so I determined to save it. I ran down the beach. My lungs screamed for air, and my heart pounded like the breakers nearby. I wondered what force had flung the ray upon the sand, leaving it gasping for breath.

Suddenly a sea gull, sailing overhead, spied the stranded ray. It soared past me, pumping its wings and squawking. It reached the ray long before I did. I screamed when it flew up into the sky, hovered, then plunged down, piercing the soft body with its bill. Again and again it rose up and plunged down.

I waved my hands, but the gull ignored me. I cried out, but the wind blew the sound away. When I reached the ray, the gull screeched at me, circled, then flew away. I stared down at what remained of the beautiful creature. There was nothing left to do but bury it and continue down the beach.

The image of that butchered ray lingered in my mind. "I feel like that ray," I whispered to God. "I'm stranded on the dry, hot sands of discouragement. Satan is plunging dagger after dagger of fear into my heart."

Suddenly I looked up and gasped. Far down the beach another ray thrashed on the sand.

"Not again!" I screamed. Then as I ran to save the stranded ray, I realized that part of my agony was not for the ray but for myself.

When I reached the ray, I immediately tried scooting it toward the water with my feet, but it thrashed its body about wildly.

I'll grab it by the tail and fling it into the water, I thought, then remembered the poison-tipped barbs and drew my hand back. The ray gasped. "What can I do?" I cried out to God. Then an idea leaped into my mind. I jerked off the shirt that covered my swimsuit, folded it into a thick square, dropped it over the tail, and grabbed the ray. Lifting the writhing creature from the sand, I held it suspended in midair and headed for the water. "Don't be afraid!" I cried to it. "I've reached you in time. I can get you to the safety of the water."

But the ray flailed its wings at my bare legs, lurching and twisting his body in a desperate attempt to free itself from my grasp.

I staggered on.

Gathering my last bit of strength, I flung it into the sea. It landed with a splat, then disappeared into the depths. I fell onto the dry sand and wept.

After a long time I sat up. I stared at the water. A thought rolled in with one of the waves and grabbed me. *Was Jesus running down the beach of my life crying out, "Don't be afraid! I will reach you in time! I will bring you to safety!"*

Another thought tumbled in. *He will never leave you nor forsake you. You feel lost and alone, but in reality you belong to God just as you always have.* The wave beat itself out on the shore and slithered up the beach as white foam. I could hear the bubbles popping as they disappeared into the sand. I felt the smallest flicker of joy as I considered the miracle of the reds, blues, and golds reflected in each tiny bubble.

"You are the Water of Life," I sighed. "Can You meet my needs and bring joy back into my heart?"

"Yes, yes, yes!" each pounding wave cried. "Yes! He is able. Trust Him!"

I had no idea what plans He could possibly have for me nor how He could put my life together, but I determined to stop thrashing about and make a firm decision to put my trust in Him as I had always done before. Though I received no flash of light or sudden answers to my problems, the fear that clutched me loosened its hold.

*Was Jesus running down the beach
of my life crying out, "Don't be afraid!
I will bring you to safety?"*

Taking Away the Power of Fear

Time passed. The fear crept back, strangling my courage and faith.

"It's fear that's paralyzing you," a voice whispered to me one morning as I knelt in prayer, trying to fight back the flood of emotions that swept over me. "Doubt and fear are between us like black clouds."

I flung myself onto the floor. *Can this be true?* I asked. *I've never been a fearful person. I know You love me. I've always known it. You have always forgiven me my mistakes. Your love is with me.*

The more I thought about it, though, the more I realized that fear was my problem. Now that I was divorced, I had to support myself. I had to find a new life. I was afraid I would fail. Although I knew Jesus love me, I had lost confidence during the past difficult months. I decided to write down the things that frightened me:

I am afraid that:

1. God is not pleased with me anymore.
2. I don't belong to anyone.
3. I'm no longer a valuable person.
4. I will fail financially.
5. I won't be able to start a new, meaningful life.

Even as I wrote, Satan screamed, Ha! It's true. You're nothing. Even your husband has discarded you. You've lost everything. Some of your friends have stopped coming around. You aren't one of the "beautiful" people anymore. You're nothing, I tell you! How can you teach people about God when you are a failure yourself? No one will ever listen to you again. Ha, ha, ha! And you thought God would solve everything. You thought God loved you.

These thoughts, my enemy, fastened themselves upon me like a cancer that had a life of its own. I knew they were lies, but the feelings of fear they evoked hung over me. When I prayed, the thoughts and the feelings faded; then, uninvited, they stomped right back into my mind at different times of the day.

Although my friends, my kids, and the church family stood with me, I still felt isolated. The scream of negative words followed me like a recording: *You think God loves you, but look at you!*

"But those are lies," I screamed back. "The Bible says, 'I will never leave you nor forsake you.' 'Those who turn to the Lord for help will not be disappointed.' 'You are accepted in the Beloved.'" The war raged for weeks—the sneering voice of my enemy, and the reasoning voice of my God.

Then one morning I decided I could not endure the battle any longer. I fell on my face in my living room and poured out a torrent of words, expressing my fears, my anger, and confusion. Hours later, I felt completely empty. No more words came.

In the silence, I considered my options: Continue to listen to the negative thoughts and allow them to grow; or make the determined choice to turn from them and throw myself on the mercy of God, receiving His power to overcome.

I choose to reaffirm my belief and love for God, in spite of appearances to the contrary, and threw my helpless self into His hands. I made no demands on Him. I stopped begging, murmuring, and pouring out my pain. I simply gave Him permission to do whatever He wanted to do with my life.

I decided not to hate and blame. It was a terrible battle because something inside me wanted to rehearse the griefs I had experienced. But I knew that I had to let go of this if God were to fill me with something better. I thought of my husband who, like me, was searching for love and meaning. I would leave him to God to fix, and I would focus on the future. Bitterness would not claim me. I would choose to offer forgiveness rather than condemnation.

Then there was nothing left to do but sit in silence.

And, slowly—almost imperceptibly at first—peace oozed up around me like a tide returning to the dry shore. It grew in depth and power until I felt enveloped in it like a crystal sea of peace. It felt so real I wanted to reach out and touch it, but I held my breath, fearing it would disappear if I did.

Feeding the Joy

I realized that this was more than an idea, a belief, or a decision. It was something tangible. I could taste it—sweet and salty as the mist from the sea. Then the peace turned into a brilliant joy, surging over me in waves. I held onto it, wanting to enjoy the moment, for I didn't think it could last. But it continued all day. And the next day. And the next.

I didn't want the joy to fade away like a brilliant sunset, so I decided to feed the joy and starve the fear. It was one of the best decisions I have ever made.

First, I daily cast myself into the hands of a loving and trustworthy God, whose compassion knows no bounds, whose promises could not fail, and whose peace was real.

Second, I learned to shut out the negative voices, refusing to let them play again and again. When they came back, I said no. Sometimes I had to pick up a nature book and gaze on the beautiful things God created, reminding myself that I was one of His creatures. Often I read the Bible, continuing until the negative voices faded. I cut out all TV, secular music, and especially the news, refusing to look at the tirade of murders, sick relationships, and disasters.

Third, at the urging of my son, David, *I practiced speaking only the hopeful words I believed and had read in the Word.* When negative thoughts came into my mind, I countered with positive words. I talked hope, repeated God's promises out loud. So many times I wanted to burst out with a tirade of my woes, but I hated the feelings that always followed.

I noticed a change almost immediately, so I persisted. The negative thoughts subsided, and peace persisted.

Fourth, I took time to express my hurt to God and remind Him of His promises, not wanting to ignore my pain. I talked with a trusted Christian friend and came to understand that I was moving through the steps of grief.

I filled my life with beauty, thinking of myself as a damaged plant that needed light, food, and water to thrive again. I did things that brought healing into my life—wandering the lake shore, watching the sun rise, and listening to the birds sing in the garden. I took time to touch the flowers, letting their sweet scents minister to me. I didn't feel like doing these things, yet as I did them my feelings changed. I made a list of those things that lifted my spirits, and I carried it around with me. This is my list:

Positive Steps I Will Take:

1. Listen to upbeat, cheerful music.	Avoid negative or mournful music of all kinds.
2. Read positive books.	Leave sad stories, cheap novels, and violence alone.
3. Turn off the TV.	Avoid endless news reports, sitcoms, movies that feature disaster, immoral actions, violence, and sadness.
4. Get outdoors.	I will swim, walk, study, draw, photograph, and enjoy.
5. Talk hope.	I will remember the ways God has helped me in the past.
6. Talk about Jesus.	I will explore the real Jesus with those who know Him.
7. Help someone.	Find someone who needs a skill I have.
8. Journal.	I will write about positive things I see, learn, and experience.
9. Listen.	Go where the sounds of laughter and nature can be heard.
10. Choose positive friends.	Avoid people who drag me down; help them later.

A faithful and wise God dealt with me where I hurt most—the

feelings of utter abandonment and fear of the future. He showed me that although I felt abandoned, I wasn't. He reminded me that He would "never leave me nor forsake me." In uncertainty, He is certain. Once I grasped the security of that idea the overwhelming pain subsided.

Your **Fight Against Fear**

It's Satan's desire to convince you through the painful circumstances that surround you that God is either unhappy with you for your mistakes, or that He doesn't love you because He has allowed this to happen to you. This is a lying ploy of Satan, designed to drive you into discouragement, anger, and sin. He knows unbelief and despair loosen your hold on Jesus, who is your only hope.

You may respond to a crisis with despondency, or you might burn with anger and bitterness. The results are the same. Both responses prod you into destructive, sinful behavior that further ensnares and brings deeper despair. This was the experience of Mary.

My choices allowed God to push the darkness away and replace negative fears with courage. In fact, soon I wanted to become bold in my belief in His love and plan for my future. So I searched for a way to strengthen my choice to trust God. I discovered King David's own personal formula that brought him boldness in the face of fear and adopted it as my battle plan.

The formula is simple, and it brings results. The reason is that God's power is behind the three actions you will discover in this formula.

Do It Anyway

Before you jump into this experience, let me caution you about two things. First, you probably won't feel like doing any of the things that make this formula work. They aren't things you naturally want to do. But do them out of choice, asking God for power.

Second, the results won't come immediately. You will have to persist when you see no results. Your experience will be a bit like an experiment I made years ago in chemistry lab. My instructor showed me how to combine hydrogen and oxygen to produce water. At first only tiny droplets of water formed on the sides of the beaker, but soon I could tip it up and take a swallow. I have never forgotten the delight I felt at that first success.

The results of this formula will seem minuscule at first, but keep going. A formula is about adding specific ingredients that will bring desired results. It's about cause and effect. It is about the coming into your life of a real person, the Holy Spirit. It is not about feelings, yet your feelings change with His presence in your life. Take a look at the formula for Fearlessness:

> "Be gracious to me, O God,
>   because I'm being constantly pressured . . . from all sides.
>   Every day [are] new ways to oppose me.
>   They are proud to fight against me.
>   Whenever I'm afraid, I will trust you.
>   I'll feed on your holy word and praise you.
>   Then my fears will subside" (Psalm 56:1-4).

First, notice the situation. David, a mighty warrior hiding in a desert cave, trying to avoid the searching eyes of wicked king Saul and his army, has been promised the kingdom. But he sees no possible way to claim it. He is under great pressure.

Next, take a look at the feelings that David admits having. He feels afraid. He admits it.

Then discover the three actions that he decides to take, in spite of his fear: He decides to trust God, to feed on God's Word, and to praise Him.

Keep in mind that every one of these actions is a choice. These verses don't say that David felt like trusting God. He probably felt like figuring out a plan to put an end to his trouble. They don't tell you that he felt like praising God; he felt afraid. And David must have been busy organizing the troops that hid with him, but he stopped and fed upon God's Word. He didn't nibble at it—he fed as one who felt a deep hunger. You can see how his feeding on the Word increased his trust in God, and that his feelings changed.

In spite of his fear, David took action in these three ways, and these actions caused his fears to subside. As panic and fear disappeared, God moved in his behalf. He did receive the promised kingdom, and his faith in God grew considerably.

This is what you want.

Consider the circle below. It shows how God works in your mind and heart as you make these choices.

What I Focus On

My Focus

My Thoughts

My Decisions
and actions

My Feelings

If you want to change your actions, you must change your focus. What you choose to focus on and talk about results in thoughts. These thoughts evoke feelings. When you take action and make choices, you are influenced by these feelings, whether positive or negative. Choosing to look at the positive truth that God loves you and is in control of your future initiates positive thoughts, and these thoughts evoke positive feelings. In turn, these feelings, firmly based upon hearing the words of truth from His word, will help you to take the action of placing your complete trust in God. The circle goes around and around.

It is true that actions should not be based upon negative feelings and that these feelings should not be the basis of your choices and decisions. However, it is also true that positive feelings will result from focusing upon the Word of God, and feelings that are based upon the truth of His love are important. Peace, joy, and comfort are feelings, and they are real when based upon the fact of His promises.

That's why God wants to be in control of your feelings. When you to focus on His promises, think about His great love, receive His peace and hope, then your actions will follow. What you say has power to make changes in your mind and heart. Words are powerful. That's why God says to sing His praises even before you receive the help you pray for.

Satan understands these truths, too. He makes a determined effort to get you to focus on your sin or your trouble. You think about it all the time. You begin to feel hopeless, guilty, confused, sad, and angry. Then you take the wrong action, make the wrong decision, and become further mired in the mud of discouragement. It is God who breaks into your view, displays His great love to your wondering eyes, fills your thoughts with hope, and gives you the feeling of peace and joy.

You make the choice to trust Him. Your faith grows. Surrounded by His covering of love, like the Angel Wing you remain unstained by further sin and negative attitudes, even when they are all around you. It is a new, miraculous life that you now experience. Fear loses its hold upon your mind and heart

Begin now! Focus on the truth. Think about it. Mull it over in your mind.

Six Reasons You Can Trust Jesus

God Knows Your Needs. According to Hebrews 4:13-16 there are six reasons you and I can trust that Jesus knows what you need:

* He sees everything and knows everything.
* He is our high priest.
* He understands how we feel because Jesus lived here.
* He was tempted more than we are being tempted.
* He never sinned.
* He now sits in heaven, beside God.

Based on these facts, there are actions you and I can take and choices that we can make. You and I can choose to:

* Hold firmly to faith in Him.

❋ Approach God with confidence.

❋ Ask for mercy and grace.

Starve your fear by feeding on God's word. Let the feelings of joy and hope take hold of your heart. Consider each word as a special gift to you by One who knows your needs.

"The Lord keeps an eye on everything that goes on in this world. He strengthens the hands of those who love Him and are loyal to Him" (2 Chron. 16:9).

"O Lord, you have searched my heart and know me inside and out. You know when I sit down when I rise; you discern my thoughts before I think them. You walk beside me all day long, and when I lie down at night, you're there. You know everything I do and say" (Psalm 139:1-3).

"The Lord looks down from heaven and observes the doings of men. From where He is, He sees us all and tenderly watches over His own. He who created us sees everything we do" (Psalm 33:13-15).

"Your heavenly Father knows your needs before you even ask" (Matthew 6:8).

God is *ready, willing,* and *able* to *help* you. Outline the facts that are meant to convince you that He is able and willing to help you in whatever situation you find yourself.

Hebrews 1:1-3 promises that He is willing and able because:

He speaks to me through His Son, Jesus.

He created me.

He shows me what God is really like.

He holds the whole universe (including me) together.

His word is powerful.

He has saved me from the power of sin.

I have a Friend in the heavenly palace.

Choose to focus on these powerful, positive facts! Ask God for the power to stay with your decision. Remember, your job is to choose, and His work is to empower you. This wonderful truth makes me feel like jumping up and down right now, as I write about it! God gives power as you choose His way. He goes to work, erasing your fears and replacing them with joy and peace.

Positive Steps Just for You

Now that you have turned your attention from your fears, focus on the positive steps you can take, with God's power. When I came to this place in my experience, I wrote out a list of what I would choose to focus on. I said, "I will focus on these positive things, even when I don't feel like it."

Make your own list, including things that will be special to you. (Remember: Focus is a choice. The power comes from Jesus.)

Here's my Positive Focus List:

1. Sing. I remember singing while tears ran down my cheeks. But it emptied out the grief and soothed my soul.

2. Plant a flower. You won't feel like it, but go ahead! Breathe deeply. Smell the fragrance from the flower. Touch the delicate petals. Look at the vivid colors. Listen to the birds in the bushes nearby. Now visualize the One who created all this as looking at you and caring for you, His flower.

3. Laugh. Read a funny book and laugh. For a few moments you will forget your troubles. These moments will come more often and will last longer. The amazing thing is that your heart can hold grief and laughter at the same time. One will ease, and the other strengthen as time goes on.

4. Praise God. Yes, thank Him for something, anything. Praise Him for what He is about to do in your life. Praise Him for who He is and what He is like. Praise Him because you can still breathe. God calls praise a sacrifice—and it is, especially when you would rather cry.

5. Take one positive step. Do something physical. Rake the yard, clean out your closets, paint the bedroom. Activity will recharge your batteries and make you feel better. You will gain a sense of pleasure from accomplishing even a small useful task. "Do just one positive thing each day," my friend, Anita, said. "It will snowball into many more, but start with just one." Good advice! You won't feel like it, but do something anyway. Your feelings will change.

6. Read the Word. Open the Word and persist at reading it. At first your mind might wander, but keep reading. You might say, "These are just words. I need real help." Read on! Start with the Gospels, taking note of His promises. Like seeds, His words will take root in your heart and produce a living harvest of hope.

7. *Help someone.* Your fears might start screaming, but remember that God is in control and is working out a solution. Ask God to show you someone you can help. Reach out to them. (Keep in mind that this is not the time to counsel a deeply-troubled person who needs professional help.)

8. *Walk.* Walking works miracles. In the midst of my trouble I wore ruts in the path that led around a small lake near my home. At first I poured out my feelings to my friend, Martha, but soon she guided our conversations to hopeful subjects. Exercise washed out the adrenalin that poured into my system and helped me to sleep better. God used squirrels, beavers, trees, and the sky to sooth my heart.

9. *Talk With God.* Go ahead—scream, cry, moan, shake your fist—whatever. He invites you to the one place you can let your heart bleed. He accepts you as you are. Slowly, persistently, powerfully, He will move you toward submission and trust. But it always will be OK to tell Him how you feel. I remember the day I realized my prayers sounded less like the moaning of a wounded bird and became more like the freedom cry of a soaring eagle who trusted in the lift of the wind beneath its wings. Praise grew, and pleadings gave way to trust.

10. *Determine to know Him.* What I already knew and experienced with God certainly saved me from utter despair, but I wanted to know more. I wanted to see Him as He really is. I felt a deep hunger to experience everything He could offer me in a personal relationship. I asked, "What are You *really* like?"

11. *Eat right.* If there is ever a time you need the best possible food, it is now. During a crisis you might want to eat everything in sight. So keep nourishing food nearby so you won't be tempted to stuff yourself with junk food. If you are one of the few who doesn't want to eat anything, you will need to ask a friend to keep an eye on you to make sure you get what you need. This is no time to go on a diet; just concentrate on eating right.

How to Let Go of Fear

A crisis or failure can send fear sweeping over you like a great wave, pounding the hope and joy right out. It can nibble at the edges of your mind, destroying your peace and sense of security, then stomp right in, demanding your full attention. Fear alters your mood then paralyzes you, making it almost impossible to take positive steps or listen to the hopeful words of others. Fear breeds first doubt, then anger, which can grow until it destroys health and makes you vulnerable to dozens of diseases and miseries. Fear has terrible power, but there is One who can snatch you out of its grip.

One day someone asked me, "How much time do you want to give to your fears, and how much power do you want your grief to have over you?" I was amazed at the question and gave it some serious thought. I decided to shift my gaze, to pry my eyes off my instant reality and look forward. I made this decision every time fear tried to push itself into my view.

What About You?

You've taken time to look at your loss and your fear, admitting that it hurts, that things will probably not ever be the way they once were. You have honestly talked with a trusted friend or counselor. Now deliberately turn, placing your back to your fear and your grief. Make the choice to turn around and face Jesus, transferring your fears and pain into His nail-scarred hands. Gaze full into the face of the One who loves you. You will have to make this decision again and again, but it will become easier and easier until you realize that your fear has subsided, and you are truly free.

When God sweeps fear from your heart,
it leaves room for Him to reveal Himself to you
in new and deeper ways.

CHAPTER FOUR

The Choice

I would not leave Him. Without the sun, the world would be black as night. Without Jesus, I would walk in darkness.

MARY CHOSE JESUS

"Deborah, look! Isn't that Mary . . ." her voice dropped, "the prostitute?"

"Shh! She'll hear you. Besides she isn't a—."

"Well, I hope she doesn't come here. I don't want anyone to see me talking to her. No matter what *you* say, once a prostitute, always a prostitute. Some things just don't change."

"The only thing that doesn't change, Hannah, is that we have to keep drawing water from this well. Here, grab that end of the rope. This is heavy."

The two women struggled to fill both water jars, then sat down in the shade of a nearby olive tree to rest. They watched Mary come along the path then stop and look into the bushes.

"What's she *doing,*" Hannah whispered.

"She's watching the black-headed buntings in those bushes. Their chests are like golden sunlight."

"I told you she was coming this way," Hannah hissed as Mary turned and headed toward the well.

"Let's get going." Hannah stood up and picked up her jar. Her jaw was set in a hard line.

"Shhh," Deborah whispered. "It's too late."

"Good morning, Hannah, Deborah," Mary said. Her smile lit her whole face. "Good morning, Mary," Deborah returned the greeting. Eyes down, Hannah fiddled with her robe but said nothing.

Mary tied the rope to her water pot and lowered it into the well. Both women watched in silence.

"Isn't it a wonderful day," Mary asked rhetorically. "I saw chicory and cumin in bloom just beyond the path where the buntings sit in the bushes and sing." Deborah nodded and Hannah pretended to adjust the sash at her waist.

With long, practiced strokes, Mary drew her pot from the well and lifted it to her shoulder. "I wish I could stay and visit," she said. "But the rabbi Jesus is visiting again, and Martha uses a lot of water when she fixes one of her feasts."

Deborah nodded sympathetically and murmured something about work never being done.

"I can't wait to get back." Mary said as she turned toward town. "I know I'm missing an interesting story right now."

Hannah made a face at Mary's back and glowered at Deborah. "Who does she think she is flouncing around acting like—"

"Like one of us?" Deborah asked quietly.

Mary stopped in mid-stride. She turned, and placed her water pot on the ground.

"Yesterday Jesus told a story about a tiny lamb called Thistle," she said, smiling at the startled women. "The lamb that got its name because the shepherd had to rescue it twice from a brier patch where those terrible spiked Syrian thistles grow.

"One night the lamb wiggled its way under the sheep gate after the shepherd had closed it for the night," she continued, not waiting for an invitation to go on.

"It danced about in the moist grass and ran freely over the hillside. Finally it wandered beyond the shepherd's land into the hills. But, when the path disappeared the lamb became confused. Soon it lost its way completely and fell, exhausted, against a large boulder.

"Then what happened?" Deborah asked, stepping closer to Mary.

"Blown by a cold wind, clouds covered the moon and blacked

out the stars. High on the mountain a wolf howled." She'd dropped her voice to a whisper. Her face held the fright of the small lost lamb. "Then came another howl," she whispered, "from the meadow below. And a long howl just beyond the great rock where Thistle huddled in the darkness, whimpering. Its whole body shook."

Deborah covered her mouth with her hand to push back a scream. Hannah sat her pot on the grass and crept to Deborah's side. She stared at Mary with wide eyes.

"The lamb stood up and peered into the night. His little ears heard the clicking-scratch of wolves running over the rocks and through the dry grass. They were coming closer, and the little lamb knew it. The wolves howled again. This time their wild blended voices came from somewhere nearby.

"The lamb saw two eyes, glowing gold in the darkness. Then the full form appeared, fangs dripping saliva. It dashed forward and grabbed Thistle by its leg. More eyes glowed in the darkness. Eyes everywhere! Thistle screamed. For an instant, the wolf dropped its hold. The lamb collapsed to the ground, and the wolf pack crept forward, snarling.

Then a voice rose above the guttural growls and snarls. "Thistle, Thistle," it called. "Thistle! Where are you?"

It was the voice of the shepherd. Thistle heard it. The wolves heard it too, and for a moment stood still. But, driven by hunger and the scent of blood, they turned again toward the trembling lamb.

"No!" Hannah cried. "They didn't kill Thistle, did they?"

"They certainly wanted to," Mary said with a long, hard look at Hannah. "They wanted to."

"Go on," Deborah pleaded.

"Suddenly the shepherd burst over the hilltop. Shouting at the top of His voice and swinging His hooked staff, he charged. The pack snarled and snapped. Eyes burning hatred, some held their ground. Ignoring the danger, the shepherd pushed himself between the pack and the lamb. One by one the wolves slunk away into the night.

"'Thistle,' the shepherd murmured, kneeling over the wounded lamb. "'It's all right, now. See, there are no wolves to hurt you. They have gone.'

Tears filled Mary's eyes, spilled over, and she wiped them away with her hand. Even so, her gaze held the two women who now clung to each other and waited.

"The shepherd tore strips of cloth from his own robe," Mary continued, "and wrapped them around Thistle's wounded leg. Then gently picking it up, He said, 'I am here. I am holding you. Don't be afraid.'

"All the way down the hillside Thistle snuggled into its savior's arms. Just as the full moon burst from behind a cloud, they reached the sheep fold. The shepherd placed the wounded lamb on a bed of dry grass. He covered it with his own outer garment, speaking words of comfort and stroking the tangled fur.

"I bet that lamb never wants to be far from the shepherd now," Deborah sighed.

"No, not ever," Mary agreed. After a long silence, she picked up her jar. "Come with me," she said. "Come hear Jesus."

"I might do that—I—" Deborah stammered.

Mary smiled, turned, and walked down the path toward town while Deborah and Hannah stared after her."

"The story was about her," Deborah said, still looking at Mary's retreating form.

Hannah pried her eyes from Mary's back and looked at Deborah. "She seems different," she said.

"Different?" Deborah asked, turning to Hannah. "Why, she's a brand new person. Did you see the softness in her eyes and the way she looked at us without a bit of hatred or bitterness even though she must have known we were talking about her? Couldn't you see the joy glowing from her eyes when she spoke of the shepherd? And you say she's only different."

Hannah shrugged and shouldered her water pot. The two women walked in silence down the winding path toward a cluster of small houses.

Throughout the months that followed, Mary became known as the one who could be found sitting at the feet of Jesus, absorbing His every word. Near Jesus she felt secure and strong. She felt loved.

They Stayed Near Him

Women down through the ages have discovered that choosing Jesus as Helper and Friend is the best decision of their lives. Once He swept fear away, their hearts filled with a longing to draw nearer to Him and to seek His help in every struggle.

Jesus' mother, Mary, chose to turn to Jesus when she became aware of a crisis in the kitchen at a wedding feast. It was the third day of what was a week-long celebration, and they had run out of wine. Immediately Mary sought Jesus' help. Without understanding how He could possibly solve the problem, she told the servants to listen to Him and do whatever He commanded (John 2:1-11). Soon, instead of water, the stone water pots overflowed with sweet fresh juice.

Among the disciples who sat beside Jesus on the hillsides, a group of women lingered. They helped with the cooking and laundry and they listened to his words. They followed Him along pathways that edged Galilee, wandered through vineyards, and climbed into fishing boats whose sails filled with wind. Always, they listened. They wanted to be near Him because in His presence something miraculous happened to them.

Look at Matthew 9:18-26. Here are the stories of two people in great need who determined to draw near to Jesus. Let their stories explode before you and melt your own reluctance to draw near Him.

Jairus, a rabbi known and admired by many, pushed through the clot of people and fell at the feet of Jesus. "My daughter is dead," he cried. "But if You come and put Your hand on her, she will live."

Immediately Jesus set out for Jairus' home. The people, eager to see another wonderful miracle, followed.

Then, unexpectedly, another story intrudes into this one. A woman whose hopes for healing have been blasted again and again, staggered behind the crowd. She, like Jairus, knew Jesus was her only hope. Again and again, she struggled to push through the crowd and draw near to Him, but it formed a human wall between them. Weakened by anemia and her futile efforts to reach Jesus, she felt almost overwhelmed by despair. She trembled. She wept. But she wouldn't give up. Like Jairus, she pressed forward.

And Jesus, already knowing her struggle, moved closer to her. In one final thrust, using every bit of strength she possessed, she reached out and touched the fringe on the edge of his garment. And life—like a surging fountain—flowed into her and throughout her body.

Two sufferers caught in impossible situations. Two people, urged forward by their need. Two strangers who—when their circumstances got even worse—made the best decision of their lives. Both of them, the rabbi and the woman, pressed closer. And they received the gift of life.

Life in One Look

The Word of God tells the stories of those who looked and lived as well as those who refused to look. You will find one of these adventures in Numbers 21. Put yourself into this ancient story.

You stand outside your tent staring at your neighbor who has just flung herself onto a mat in front of her tent doorway. Sari's groans tell you that she's been bitten by a desert serpent and the poison is doing its deadly work. You weep because there is no antidote for the snakebite, and there is nothing you can do for her.

Moses, leader of the people, has sent messengers to each family warning everyone to beware of the outburst of serpents throughout the encampment. He has asked the people to pray to the God of Israel for protection and healing. Even now, Moses and the elders are meeting at the tabernacle and praying for God's intervention.

You sigh. You realize that your loving God has protected you and your people from these serpents for the more than 20 years you've lived in the great desert. But many began to grumble and complain about God's dealings with them. You shudder at the results of their rebellion, at their accusations that God has not taken care of them. Despite His protection from wild animals, despite the water God provided, and the manna He sent every morning, most of the people accuse God of bringing them to the desert to die.

So God withdrew His protection from the snakes that were always there. Already many of your neighbors are dead from snakebite, and the whole encampment is in a panic.

Suddenly another messenger arrives, breathless. "God spoke to Moses! He commanded him to make a bronze serpent, place it on a

pole, and put it in the middle of the camp. God promised that anyone who looks at the serpent will live. Look!" the man cries. "You
can see the bronze serpent from here!" And he is gone, dashing to
the next tent.

A serpent on a pole? How can that help? Then understanding
comes. You remember God's promise to send His Son, Jesus, to die
for your sins. Jesus is to be lifted up on a cross. He will become sin
for you. The serpent on the pole represents Jesus becoming sin, and
giving His own life for you. Just as you must look to Him for salvation—for your very life—if you look upon the symbol of Christ-
made-sin-for-you, you will be saved.

You glance at your neighbor stretched out on the mat, her body
trembling from the poison coursing through it. Her daughter bends
over her, stroking her hair and crying. *If she could just choose to look at
the pole and the serpent, she would be healed—just as God promised,* you
think. You rush to her side.

"Sari, look up!" you scream, shaking the woman awake. "Look
at the serpent on the pole. You will live!"

"She's right!" the daughter cries. "If you look, you'll live. Oh,
Mother, I need you. Please look."

Sari stirs on the mat, her face contorted with pain. You squat beside her and lift her to a sitting position, turning her head toward the
pole, and wiping her swollen eyes with the hem of your robe.
"Open your eyes," you plead. "It's God's promise. He's the only
One who can help you."

The woman's eyelids flicker. They open. She strains to focus on
the pole that stands just within her sight. Knots of people surround
it. Some lie on mats, others kneel about them, begging. The word
on every tongue is "Look!"

"I see it," Sari whispers, her voice thin and trembling. "I see the
serpent."

"Mother, the serpent is a picture of our God who saves," the
daughter whispers into her ear.

You watch as Sari stares at the serpent. Suddenly she wrenches
free of your grasp and leaps to her feet. "I'm healed! I'm well!" she
shouts, throwing herself into her daughter's arms. They cling to each

other, laughing and praising God.

Suddenly you feel possessed by a desire to help others. You run to the next tent, crying out, "Look! Look and live!" Then, you run on. The sun burns overhead. It dips and slips toward the desert horizon. Shouts of joy and cries of sorrow mingle together and fill the air. For life or death—each person has made their decision. Obey, look at the Life-giver and live, or refuse to look and die.

My Most Important Decision

"You must call all the people on this list," my boss, Dr. Davidson said, thrusting a paper into my hands. "Each of these couples is waiting for a baby to adopt, and one has just become available. It's a little girl."

I thought of the wonderful little boy, Stephen, God had given me, who slept snugly at home. I knew I must find a place for the tiny girl who had no home, but slept in a hospital crib. But two days later I had reached the bottom of the list and still hadn't found a family willing to give the baby a home.

"Why don't you take her," Dr Davidson asked. "You have so much love to give. I hate to send her off to an orphanage."

"A person just doesn't take a baby home every day of the week," I objected, thinking of our small apartment already bursting with baby equipment. Where would we put another crib? How could we make room for a new child? After I graduated from the nursing class, I had signed up for extra classes. And too, my husband still had one year of studies. Taking in a little one seemed like an impossible dream.

Then I thought of our neighbors downstairs. I smiled to myself remembering the scent of freshly baked bread that wafted up into our apartment every Monday. I had gone downstairs one morning to see who was creating such a delicious aroma and there stood Mr. May, pulling a loaf of fresh bread from the oven. "How did you do that," I said, looking into his blank eyes.

"You mean, how does a blind man bake?" he asked with a smile. "Nothing's impossible."

"That man does amazing things," his wife said, coming into the room.

68

I had soon learned that not only could he bake bread, he cleaned the house and helped with the grocery shopping. I got used to hearing his footsteps coming up the steep stairway each afternoon.

"Mary and I are going to town for a few things," he always said. "Can we get you anything?"

I wanted to talk with these friends who seemed to have conquered life's challenges. "Nothing is impossible," I could hear Mr. May say, smiling through unseeing eyes.

"An orphanage? How terrible," my husband said when I called home at lunch time. "Surely we can squeeze this little girl into our lives. I'll meet you after your sanctuary class," he told me, "and we can pick the baby up at the hospital." I was thrilled. "Oh, don't forget," he added, "you need to pick out a name."

My head was swirling with thoughts as I hurried to class. When I slipped into my usual front row seat, my mind was far away. Could this be happening to me? I was going to have a baby, right now. Today! We did want a little girl to complete our family, but adoption was unplanned. God certainly had good ideas, and He worked very fast. He was giving me another child to love. I smiled to myself and scribbled out a note. "Need a girl's name for a newborn," it said.

I slipped the note to Carol, the girl on my right. She wrote something down, then passed it on to her neighbor. The note flew around the room. Names were added and some marked off.

Suddenly the teacher, Dr. Harding, swirled around. Pointing to me, he asked, "Sally, what is going on here."

Startled by his question, I blurted out, "I'm going to have a baby today." Every eye in that room turned and fastened itself on my stomach.

"I'm adopting one," I explained.

Dr. Harding asked for the note. He looked at it, than wrote the list of names on the board. We voted. The baby's name would be Susie.

The next six weeks passed in a flurry of shopping, showing off the baby and adjusting to another child in our tiny apartment. Susie passed her six-week checkup with flying colors and that night I put her to bed feeling good that she was thriving and growing as she should.

Suddenly sunlight burst through the window, and I sat up. I had overslept. My husband had already left for school. Stephen lay curled up in his crib, sleeping. I ran to the bassinet and peeked in at Susie. She lay still. Wow! I had just slept a whole night without interruption. I felt wonderful.

I put my hands under her little arms and lifted her up into the light streaming into the room. "Good morning, little sunshine," I said.

I stared at her. She was dead! Her face had flattened out on one side and looked blackened. I screamed and dropped her into the bed. Stephen awoke in the next room and cried. I ran from the house, screaming.

Mr. May groped his way up the stairs and into our apartment. I stood, waiting for some miracle. Surely Susie was alive. But he came out and stumbled down the stairs. "I am afraid she's dead," he said, shaking his head.

"There's nothing you could have done," the doctor told me after examining Susie. "It's a case of SIDS, sudden infant death syndrome. She just stopped breathing."

Death of a Dream

It seemed the entire campus mourned with us as we placed Susie into the tiny casket and bore her to the cemetery. A dream died inside me when two men lowered her into the ground. And the picture of a loving, kind, and merciful Jesus with wonderful ideas and plans that had been building in my life since girlhood, became a blur in the fog of my grief. The ghostly image of someone distant, cruel, and unpredictable stalked my dreams. How could Jesus let this happen? Why would He bring this baby into my heart and home only to snatch her away so quickly? Why, oh why, hadn't He awakened me? The fact that He let me sleep while my baby died haunted me day and night.

When I took Stephen to Sabbath school, I wept at the sight of all the little ones sitting in their chairs. Susie would never sit in one of these chairs. She would never sing a Sabbath school song. It seemed there was nothing in my experience that could help me face the unexpected fate of my innocent baby.

A Choice

One predawn morning, months later, I awoke to a sudden realization. I would have to do one of two things.

I could give up on Jesus. I could leave Him as He had left me, and forget the whole business of being a Christian.

Or I could choose to get to know Him better. I could leave judgment of my experience until I came to a better understanding concerning who He was and what I could expect from Him.

Silently considering this decision, I lay silently staring out the window into the darkness. A faint glimmer of light began to glow in the sky, and an idea was born. As the tiny pinprick of red light appeared on the horizon and grew until it became a blazing ball, my idea grew. I would not leave Him. Without the sun the world would be black as night, and without Jesus, I would walk in darkness. No. I would not leave Him.

Like a marble shot from a boy's hand, the sun burst into the sky shattering shadows and warming the air. I *will* find a way to know Him better, I decided. I will look, and my faith will live! I will press closer. A great adventure began that day and became a new way of living.

I could give up on Jesus, or I could choose to get to know Him better.

Making *Your* Choice

Like me, and just as thousands of women from every age in history, your heart contains a "measure of faith." With that measure, you must make a choice. Listen to His invitation: "Come to me, you who are tired and worried, and I will give you rest. Take up my work and learn from me, for I am gentle and kind, and you will discover an abiding peace in your soul. My requirements are easy and the load you carry will be light" (Matthew 11:28-30).

Look carefully at these powerful words. Circle the verbs, or action words, that tell you what to do.

Come to Me.

Work with Me.

Learn from Me.

Now discover the results of coming to Jesus, working with Him, learning from Him. Your life will become changed because of the science of *cause* and *effect.* Each action brings a certain result. Circle those results.

> Rest—given as a free gift.
> Peace—beyond your wildest dreams.
> A light, easy load.

When you answer Christ's invitation, you will come to Him, work and cooperate with Him, and learn about Him. While you do these things, you will be given restfulness, peace beyond human understanding. And the load He gives you to carry becomes light and easy.

Because He has forgiven your sins and given you eternal life as a gift, you now walk with Him in this way. This is the greatest adventure you will ever enter into. It will grow and become a new way of living.

One of my favorite authors, Ellen White, wrote these words.

"The Elder Brother of our race is by the eternal throne. He looks upon every soul who is turning his face toward Him as the Savior. He knows by experience what are the weaknesses of humanity, what are our wants and where lie the strength of our temptations; for He was in all points tempted like as we are, yet without sin. He is watching over you, trembling child of God. Are you tempted? He will enlighten. Are you wounded? He will heal" (*Desire of Ages,* p. 329).

"Those who take Christ at His word, and surrender their souls to His keeping, their lives to His ordering, will find peace and quietude. Nothing of the world can make them sad when Jesus makes them glad by His presence. In perfect acquiescence there is perfect rest" (*Desire of Ages,* p. 330).

A Choice That Changed My Life

At the age of 48 I became a SCUBA diver. Perhaps I made this decision to help ward off the terrors of an empty nest syndrome now that my children had started lives of their own, but it soon became a fantastic adventure in knowing God.

One morning I found myself standing before a store window. "Start Diving Lessons Now," a sign shouted. A dream, buried in the distant past, jumped into the present. I signed up.

A friend, Martha, agreed to the plan, and we joined a class with eight young people. At the end of six weeks we had learned to survive in the bottom of the sea, locate the boat, and return to the surface safely. We each received a card that said PADI, in bold letters.

Then one sunlit morning I found myself, with Martha, bumping over the sea in a dive boat, heading for the reef. I wiggled into my gear as the boat leaped over the small waves. Soon it stopped and the captain threw over the anchor. I could see the dark shadow of the reef 100 feet beyond the boat. I finished gearing up by strapping on my weight belt, knife, and computer, then staggered to the dive platform at the end of the boat and stuck my feet into my new, pink fins.

A helper grabbed me by the neck of my dive vest and held on as I teetered on the dive platform. I had made the decision to dive, taken the lessons, gathered the extensive gear, and climbed into the boat. But, I wasn't a real diver until I actually jumped off that boat and entered the water. This was the moment of truth.

"Leap!" the dive master screamed and I stuck my right foot out and propelled myself off the end of the boat. It was more of a dead drop than a forward leap, but considering the mass of heavy equipment that hung off my body, I thought myself to be a great success when I landed in the water with a splash totally intact. My dive buddy leaped right behind me, and we both pushed a button that removed all air from our buoyancy vests and felt ourselves sinking to the bottom of the sea. We had become real divers. Now we could learn, practice, and sharpen our skills. We would discover the outrageous beauty of the reef. Joy and excitement coursed through my being, and I kicked my fins and headed for a new way of experiencing life.

Choosing Jesus—A Life-changing Choice

Imagine it. Israel's Temple rings with rich, pure, joyous laughter. People have gathered in small groups, pressing close to Jesus who has drawn them like a magnet. They want to see His face and hear His words. They want to see Mary, the forgiven woman. You join them.

Perhaps you came with a troubled heart or guilty soul. Perhaps you find you are almost as afraid as Mary was when thrown at His feet, but His voice lassoes you in. You listen to every word, not taking your eyes from Him because you've never seen a face like this, brimming with undisguised love. His eyes move over the crowd. They pause on your face.

At first you feel pleased, but as He looks into your eyes it seems that He is looking into the deepest part of your heart. Terror seizes you. You want to leap to your feet and run, yet you want to stay and let Him look. Suddenly you realize that He sees all—all your guilt, all your weaknesses, all your needs. He reads your story. You suck in a deep breath. Will He reject you because of what He sees?

O God, help me. Accept me as you did Mary, you cry silently. His eyes continue to search you. And as you realize what He sees, you see love. You feel forgiveness. You know acceptance. It has only been a moment, but it will last forever. Then He looks on to other faces, searching them.

You feel knit to Him with a bond that you don't understand. A new and strange longing fills your heart. You know you are in the presence of God and that this Jesus fully knows and accepts you. He is happy to be with you. You can't speak because the wonder of it is exploding inside you.

The people who surround Jesus at this point are those who feel their need of Him. The proud and self-righteous have fled.

When He leaves the Temple, you join the crowd that follows Him along a singing brook, over hills dotted with wild flowers, and down to the sparkling Sea of Galilee. His every act is drenched with love, His every word builds hope. And all your cares are lost in a desire to be near Him.

The next morning as the sun bursts into a robin egg-blue sky, you realize that you feel a sense of fearlessness, that you feel confidence and peace. Hope dances within your heart. Your problems, resting in the hands of Jesus, have left you free—free to focus on Him.

You've looked over the reality of your circumstances, the offer of Jesus, and made your choice. You've taken the leap of faith and said yes to His call. You have come to Him. Now, get set for adventure! The amazing beauty of Jesus, the Water of Life, is before you. Kick your fins of faith and get going. Learn. Grow. Sharpen those looking skills.

*Now that you have made your choice,
your joy will grow, and your fears
and insecurity will begin to shrink.*

CHAPTER FIVE

Face-to-face With the Heart Mender

*When He won my trust He showed me
how to hide in His love through the storms.*

MARTHA LEARNS TO LISTEN

"Jesus is coming," Mary shouted. She barged into the kitchen where Martha stood at the table kneading bread dough.

"How wonderful," Martha smiled. She wiped her hands on her apron and stepped into the front room to look out the door. "Look," she said, "His disciples are with him. They'll be hungry." Her brow knit in a worried frown. "I hope you'll help me, Mary," she added.

"I'm glad to see them," her sister said, "but I'm afraid to have Him so close to the city and the scheming priests. They sit in the Temple contemplating how they can be rid of Him."

Within minutes the group had arrived. The two sisters greeted them warmly, then Mary ran to a nearby field where their brother Lazarus was working.

"Jesus is here, and He's brought His disciples. Come quickly, Lazarus," Mary called. Without waiting a heartbeat, Mary ran home. She wanted to hear what Jesus would say. The thought that she might be missing one of His stories made her sigh. Out of breath, she slipped into the room and sat down in a corner near Him.

Through an open door she could see Martha bustling about in the kitchen. She heard the sound of chopping and stirring. She heard the back door open and close. Minutes later it opened again and footsteps told her that Martha was back. *I'll get up and help her in a moment,* Mary thought. But soon she was lost in another story that held deep meaning to her.

Martha fairly flew about the kitchen. Jesus was an important guest and deserved the best. "If only Mary would help," she sputtered aloud. "Look at her, just sitting there. Why doesn't she get out here and help me? Jesus doesn't come often, and when He does I want everything to be just right." She stepped to the front room door and stood staring. *Maybe I should just ask Jesus to intervene,* she thought. Surely He cared about her problem.

"Martha," Jesus said. "Please come in and—"

"Lord, don't you care anything about how much work it takes to feed all of these men?" Martha asked, interrupting Him. "The least you can do is to tell my sister to help me."

Jesus looked at Martha with understanding. "Martha, Martha, you are helpful to everyone in need," he said. His eyes were kind, his voice gentle. "And you're going to great lengths to feed us and make us comfortable. But there are more important things than food and comfort. Mary came to me because she recognizes her need. She has done the right thing. The things I'm telling her will help her for the rest of her life."

"Yes, Lord," Martha replied. She felt embarrassed and subdued, but there was still work to do. Back in the kitchen she stood looking out the narrow window. A small vineyard stood in rows that climbed the gentle hill. Clusters of purple grapes punctuated the green leaves. Soon there would be juice, fresh and sweet.

Perhaps, she thought, *it is just as Mary said.* Looking and listening to Jesus was like being connected to the vine and producing grapes. Suddenly she missed being part of the group. She was tired. Tired of hurrying about refilling cups and gathering plates. She wanted to sit and look at Jesus, really look. She wanted to see what Mary saw and feel the peace she was certain Mary felt.

She glanced at the oven just beyond the kitchen window. The

flat bread she'd slapped on its sides must be nearly done. She'd meant to serve it with Jesus' favorite stew, but that would take most of the morning to prepare. *Perhaps I won't,* Martha decided. She smiled, pleased with her decision. Now that she wasn't making stew she could take her time, so she walked into the main room and sat beside Mary.

"I decided not to cook after all," she whispered to Mary. "I want to hear Jesus, too."

Mary looked at her with surprise, then she smiled. "And as soon as this story is over and I understand what Jesus is trying to teach, I'll help you prepare a quick meal," Mary said. The sisters clasped hands and turned toward the conversation.

Martha listened, soon losing herself in His words. She watched Jesus closely. His eyes danced with a special light, and He laughed often. She had never noticed it before. She leaned closer. She read patience and love in His eyes.

"I am the Living Water," He told them. Martha thought of water droplets distilled on the rose petals in the garden. Then she imagined a mountain stream flinging itself over a cliff and splashing down upon smooth stones in its rush toward the Sea of Galilee. She could taste its sweetness and feel the cool upon her lips.

Suddenly Martha wanted to hear every word. She felt a deep hunger inside herself.

Mary squeezed her hand. "He really *is* like water," she whispered. "Water that purifies and cleanses."

"Yes," Martha said, tears filling her eyes. He has cleansed your life and brought great joy to this house. But, Mary, He needs to cleanse me, too."

"But you never—" Mary began.

"Anything that separates us from Him is sin, Mary. It robs us of what's important and life-giving. I know that now, and I'm sorry that I let my busyness come between us."

Jesus paused in mid-sentence and looked straight at Martha. Then He flung back His head and laughed at some unseen joy.

"He knows," Martha said to her sister. "He knows."

"And those who drink of the living water will never thirst

again," He concluded.

Several disciples stood and stretched. Small conversations erupted. The two women lingered a moment longer. "Martha," her sister said, "now I'll help you serve supper."

Martha got to her feet and took a step toward the kitchen. Then she turned and caught Jesus' eyes upon her. *He knows,* she thought. *And I understand, at last.*

I Learn to "See" Him

For three days January's cold wind blew over the surface of the sea, building up walls of water then digging out deep valleys. It plunged fingers into the bay, stirring up the sand, and flung waves against the beach. It howled in the treetops and sent boat flags dancing.

On the fourth day, I awoke to silence. I dashed to the window and threw open the blinds. A pale sun peaked over the horizon and eased into the sky. I jumped into my bathing suit and ran to the water's edge. Florida's sea lay still, glistening in the morning sunbeams. I waded into the water.

"It's still cold," I mumbled, wading in deeper and shivering as the water inched up my legs. I looked down to scan the sand for shells or tiny fish, but I couldn't even see my feet. "No SCUBA diving today," I complained.

But the sea called me. I just had to get into the water. I longed to learn a new lesson from the sea and draw closer to the Creator. I hungered for the deeper connection I always felt while searching out one of God's fantastic creations. Finally, I decided to snorkel along an old rock jetty that protected the entrance of the bay from rough seas. *At the least I'll find some cowrie shells,* I thought.

I strapped on my dive knife and wiggled into my snorkel gear, then plunged into the cold water. *I'll warm up when I get some good kicking going,* I thought. The swells sloshed me about like a cork.

This wasn't going to work. I knew I'd better get out.

But just as I prepared to climb out of the water, I noticed the lacy, round shape of a fish. It lay still against the white sand not more than three feet beneath me. Two plump round eyes sat perched atop its flat head and they rolled in their sockets, both working independently of each other. Despite the murky water, I could see the iridescent purple rings that decorated its body. "It's a peacock flounder," I shouted into my snorkel. The flounder spotted me and flattened itself into the sand.

"So you think you can hide from me," I said. The flounder didn't move.

I smiled, remembering that the flounder starts life much like any other fish, with eyes on each side of its head and lips out front. But by a miracle that God invented, all that changes. The flounder turns to lie on one side. The lips stay put, but the eye that is now against the sand, migrates to the other side of the head and sits beside the other eye. This creates a weird picture.

I also remembered that flounders don't go dashing about after food. They wait until the food comes to them. *They must be very patient,* I thought.

But, I didn't feel patient. I wanted action.

I wonder how fast a flounder can slither along the sand, I thought. *I want to see it dart off like a floating pancake.* I waved my hand in the water right over its head, feeling sure the flounder would flee at top speed. To my surprise, it simply lay against the sandy sea floor. I waved both hands. The flounder snuggled deeper into the sand.

Next I reached for my dive knife strapped to my lower leg, and pressed the button. It almost jumped out of the case. I waved it back and forth near the flounder.

"You'll take off now," I laughed through my snorkel. But the flounder only glanced at me, the enemy. It didn't panic. It didn't take off. It stared at the sand. Then before my confused eyes, that flounder changed color until it perfectly matched the colors in the sand. It became like the sand and disappeared from my sight.

I know it's still there, I thought. I removed my right fin, slid it under a spot that looked like the place the fish had been and lifted it up. The flounder shook itself, glanced at me, and dove for the sand. It wiggled itself into the sand and disappeared again.

I looked at the place where I knew the flounder lay still. Two bubble eyes looked at me, but the fish lay still.

I've been taught by a fish, I thought. That flounder just showed me that I will become like what I focus on. The words of John in chapter one, verse 29, came to my mind as it reads in the King James Version: "Behold the Lamb of God which taketh away the sin of the world." Even though I know its original meaning was that of John telling the crowd around him to look at Jesus, I learned another truth from this verse. Just as the flounder stared at the sand and became like it, I can look at Jesus and become like Him. As I behold Jesus, I will come to hate sin and He will take it away. That would include fear, guilt, and even worry.

I made a decision. "I will copy you, little flounder," I whispered through my snorkel. "I will look at my Creator through His creation, and I will be changed."

Amazing Discoveries

It wasn't long before I began to see pictures of Jesus in nature. On a trip to Canada I determined to find as many pictures of Him as I could. I prayed and asked the Holy Spirit to help me discover them. I bought a notebook so I could record the adventure and the lesson, along with a Bible verse that matched. .

Rick, a real Canadian outdoors man and his wife, Joy, invited me to spend a whole day exploring the wilderness just beyond their home. I gazed at the great mountains that rimmed the expanse of prairie. I imagined Canada spread out before me like a giant county whose toes play in the waters of the Great Lakes and whose fingers reach up and clasp glaciers. I thought of the West, where towering snow capped mountains were fringed by a coastline and breakers that burst upon ragged rocks.

These pictures gave me a glimpse of God's greatness, but I wanted to learn specific lessons from individual creatures. "Show me," I whispered to God.

As we drove up over a hill, I noticed a herd of cows clustered together munching grass. A small calf nestled against the side of each mother cow. "Stop so I can get a picture," I said to Rick. He slowed and pulled off the road. The three of us climbed out and walked up to a fence that surrounded a great field.

I tried to imagine that a shepherd stood somewhere nearby, a kind and strong one who cared for these animals. Then I imagined Jesus as my shepherd, but I just couldn't get the idea to take form. I had no idea what a shepherd looked like nor what he actually did.

"Look!" Joy shouted. "That mother cow is in a panic. See how she pushes her way through the herd sniffing every calf. Listen to her bellow."

"Somehow she and her calf have gotten separated," Rick said. "I hope it isn't lost."

We searched the vast grassland with our eyes. "Maybe the calf is just lost in the herd and can't find its mother," Joy said hopefully.

"Look!" Rick shouted. "I see the calf. He pointed toward a dry creek bed that snaked its way across the prairie. A small form lay hunched up in the grass. I wanted to climb right over the fence, grab the calf and take it to its mother. "She'll find it," Rick told me, placing his hand on my shoulder.

Then I spotted a slender, brown animal trotting along just beyond the edges of the herd. It trotted with its head down, its nose close to the roots of the grass, and its tail straight out behind it.

"A coyote," Rick blurted. "He's slinking around looking for lost or wounded calves."

"Oh, no!" Joy and I cried together.

We looked back at the field. The mother cow still pressed her way through the herd searching for her calf. "She knows that coyote is nearby," Joy said.

"Where's the Shepherd?" I asked. "Why isn't he here to help these cows?" I sounded so angry that both Rich and Joy turned to look at me. I realized that they had no way of knowing the double meaning of my question.

A Bad Shepherd

"Cowboy shepherds ride herd around here," Rick said. "They watch out for strays and coyotes." His eyes scanned the vast prairie. I knew he hoped a shepherd would suddenly burst into view. And that's just what happened. Up over the low hill came a great black horse. A man sat tall in the saddle. He held his head high and his shoulders straight back. A great brimmed hat sat on his head and he wore black boots with silver spurs that caught a glint of sunlight. He looked like he owned the whole prairie.

I sighed. Suddenly I knew I was about to get my lesson. I would see a picture of a shepherd. I knew he'd discover the little calf, jump from his horse, kneel down in the wet grass and lift that frightened calf into his strong arms. He would lay it across his saddle, then mount his horse, and they'd gallop off to the herd and the worried mother. *Wow,* I thought. *This is going to be good.*

The cowboy did spot the calf, and he did leap from his horse. But he didn't kneel down beside the calf, nor pick it up in his arms. He kicked it!

I caught my breath. Joy jumped. Rick grabbed the fence post with both hands.

The calf cried out and struggled to his feet. It bounded away as fast as his wobbly legs could carry it, fleeing from those silver spurs. The cowboy leaped on his horse, they swirled around and rode up beside the calf. *Wham!* The boot and spur found the calf's side. Again and again the calf ran and dropped to the earth. Again and again the cowboy wheeled his horse around, rode up beside the calf, and gave him a kick.

"Oh, dear Father, don't let the horse trample that tiny, helpless creature," I prayed.

Finally the calf slumped to the ground in exhaustion and didn't try to get up. He didn't try to escape the boots nor the spurs.

"What's the matter with you?" I screamed over the wind that swooped across the grasses. "The Bible says that Jesus is the shepherd. But, not like that. He's kind."

"Not all cowboys are unkind like that," Rick said, looking at me. I hadn't meant to shout, but the words just burst out. My picture of a loving shepherd caring for a lost calf was ruined.

A Good Shepherd

Then suddenly from over the hillside, came another horse. Its hooves pounded the earth. A rider sat tall in the saddle. As he came near I could see his handsome, tanned face beneath his wide, white hat. His eyes scanned the prairie. He spotted the baby calf and the cowboy shepherd with the silver spurs. He frowned. Then he rode right up to that tiny calf and leaped from his horse. He reached down, scooped up the calf, brushed it off, and laid it across his saddle. I stood speechless. I stared. I felt tears coming. The cowboy led his horse toward the herd of cows then brought it to a stop. He put the calf down onto the wet grass.

"MOO!" the frantic mother cow bellowed. She burst through the herd, sniffing the air. She lifted her head and mooed. The calf heard her voice above his fear and pain. He took off in the direction of that sound. They met, nose to nose and heart to heart. The mother cow gently nudged her calf toward the herd, and they trotted off together. The cowboy reined in his horse and galloped over the prairie.

We watched until the form of the mother and her baby blended into the herd, and we watched the coyote slink into the high grass. Then Rick started up the car and we sped away.

My heart fell on its knees and I thanked Jesus for being the GOOD shepherd. I thanked Him for finding me when I felt lost and helpless. He reached down from heaven and picked me up in His strong arms and carried me to safety. He cheated the coyote, Satan, out of one more victim.

Now when I read verses that remind me of my GOOD shepherd, I see my Jesus. He's very handsome. He sits straight in the saddle. He clearly sees all His kingdom. And He rides on His white horse to victory and to my rescue. Nature in the form of a cow and her calf showed me a picture of Jesus. I had learned about trust.

His Portrait in Nature

You may be saying, "It's so hard to relate to a person I can't see and hear. It's so hard to feel close to them."

Jesus understands this so He invented a picture book with His portrait inside. Read Romans 1:20. Even though we can't actually see God, we can understand how He governs by looking at nature. It's been that way since the creation of this world. We can understand the regenerative power of God and His goodness by observing the *things He made,* and that leaves people without any excuse.

How God Teaches

God, separated from you by a chasm of sin, guilt and fear, chose to send Jesus to reveal the truth about Himself. He meant for you to see what He is like by looking at the life of Jesus, His Son.

He draws you near through Jesus.

He reaches toward you through the help of the Holy Spirit.

These three, who work together toward one purpose, bridge the gulf and connect you with heaven itself. The wonders of Creation contain portraits of your God, assisting you in your quest to connect with Him and draw near.

God's greatest challenge is to get your attention.

This is no small thing when you consider how busy you are, how consumed by troubles, concerns, and activities. God made the earth, sea, and sky full of delightful, enticing, and incredible creatures that fairly shout, "This is what I am like." They capture your attention, delight your senses, and draw you in to adventure.

I learned this principle the first time I jumped off the end of a dive boat. I hit the water with a splash and sank to the sand 40 feet below. I leveled off and kicked my fins. A kaleidoscope of colored fish swept past. They caught my attention alright. As I chased them through the reef, I saw green moray eels peek from crevices, a grouper dawdle at a cleaning station, and a peacock flounder slither beneath the sand. Although the 50 minutes of dive time disappeared like dew beneath a tropical sun, the pictures I saw will last forever. I couldn't wait to leap into the water again. That reef had my attention, and its Creator my awe. Curiosity drove me to the library where I gathered bits of information here and there on every creature I had seen. Within the experience and the study, I discovered glimpses of a Creator that amazed me. God had accomplished His first feat. He certainly had my attention!

Next, I found that after a dive I felt a delicious elation and sense of well-being. I felt love bouncing around inside me as never before. I finally realized that nature was lifting my affections to God as I saw His creativity displayed and His care for each creature. The reef became like a billboard announcing *I made these creatures and I take care of them. I can certainly take care of you.* And, I got the message.

It wasn't long before I realized that each creature had a specific lesson to teach and that these lessons matched those taught in God's word. At this point in my adventure my notebook began to fill with amazing information that later played a great part in what God would do with my future. Nothing could turn me back from this way of learning about God. I was hooked.

On my second dive I learned something else that shook me to the core. It happened because I spotted the outline of a small flounder in the sand. After seeing one on my first dive I'd been amazed by what I discovered when I researched flounders. The sight of that fish brought back every bit of knowledge, the delight of my first discovery of the fish, and the lesson it taught me. I even remembered the Bible verse I'd put with the fish: "By beholding, we become changed." Seeing the flounder again triggered all this. And since that time, whenever I see flounders, it all comes back as forceful as the first time I saw one. The response is automatic.

Nature actually anchored all this in my mind as well as my emotions. This discovery amazed me. I wanted more. I headed out to the reef as often as I could so that nature could:

> Capture my attention.
> Lift my affections to God.
> Teach me the truth about God.
> Anchor truth in my mind and heart.

God's greatest challenge is to get your attention.

Make it *Your* Miracle

It's time for you to experiment with this concept for yourself. I know you can't get out right now and jump off a dive boat, but even in a written form a nature adventure can become a bit of an experience.

Take a look at the following story and see how God uses His creation to reach into your heart and mind. Of course you would sense His power more deeply in an adventure of your own if you could taste the salty air, laugh at the fish antics, and enter into the action yourself. Nevertheless, give it a try then let it push you out the door into your own adventures. Read the story twice. The first time your curiosity will get the better of you and demand satisfaction. The second time you read the story, ask yourself these questions:

Did this sea creature capture my attention, nudging my curiosity?

Do I feel affection toward God because of the adventure?

Did I learn a truth about the Creator?

Miracle at Honaunau Bay

Honaunau Bay sat like a half moon at the foot of the mountain and shimmered in Hawaii's noonday sun. I carried my snorkel gear to the edge of the water and began to adjust my mask and slip into my fins.

"You're going to love it in there," a strange voice said to me.

I looked up. A young boy stood in front of me, a large puddle forming at his feet as water dripped from his swim trunks and a ragged t-shirt. He shoved his mask back onto his forehead, pushing a large fringe of red hair up behind it. He swiped his hand across his wet, freckled face and flashed me a grin that rivaled the sun.

"I saw the Humuhumu-nukunuku-a-pua'a," he said.

"You *what?*" I asked jumping to my feet.

"Its a little triggerfish that makes a little grunting piglike sound and has a needlelike spine. That's how he got the name Humuhumu-nukunuku-a-pua'a. It means "fish that sews and grunts like a pig."

"This is its picture," he said, holding up a plastic card with a dozen fish printed on it.

"You sure know your fish," I said, taking the card in my hands and studying the pictures.

"They're all over the place out there, but be sure to snorkel around that overhang," he told me, pointing to the right side of the bay. "I saw a little cave, and it's full of small fish. I think it's a place they can hide from predators."

"Thanks for the tip." I turned back into the water so I wouldn't trip over my finned feet.

He watched with some inner delight bursting out through his eyes. "Hey!" he added, "Watch out for that whirlpool. It's off to the far right at the mouth of the bay."

"OK," I mumbled through my snorkel, and disappeared beneath the surface.

Wow! I thought, *Visibility must be over 100 feet. This is paradise for sure.*

Rainbows of Fish

Rainbows of fish swished past me as I glided along. A gold and black Moorish idol darted past as if following its own long snout, and a fantail filefish with scaleless velvety skin twitched its fan-like tail. A thin, silver barracuda moved along beside me, staring. He shadowed me for 10 minutes before gliding off into the distance. I watched color-splashed angel fish flit here and there decorating the bay, and smiled at a shy black-banded wrasse with weird buck teeth peeking from its hiding places among the coral. It was all I could do to keep my mouth clamped around the snorkel. I wanted to shout for joy.

I want to come here every day, forever, I thought to myself. *I want to jump into this bay, kick my fins and follow the fish as they dart about. I want to laugh at the fat puffers and ooh over the colors of the butterfly fish.*

A whitespot goatfish moved along the sand below me. I gulped air, held my breath, and dove. I watched it probe the sand for food using a pair of feelers called barbels. Too soon I had to return to the surface. I grabbed a breath and headed toward shallow water to rest. When I stood up, I noticed several people removing their masks and heading for shore.

"What's up?" I called to a man nearby.

"We've just been told that a bad storm is heading this way. It could become a hurricane, and they want the bay cleared of people within the next hour or so."

I scanned the sky. In the distance I could see a great blackness moving toward the bay. It spread itself over the whole horizon.

"It's supposed to be a big one," the man said, removing his fins. "Guess I'm done for the day."

I just stood there looking out over the sea. I imagined that the black wall would shut out the sun, and the wind would whip up the waves and send them slamming against the shore. I thought the wild water might even catch those tiny fish and fling them up onto the beach where they would gasp for air, beat their fins against sand, and die.

A pain, like a knife, cut through me. *No!* I thought. Without the fish, the bay would be ruined. I'd seen shallow bays in the Bahama Islands where great storms had churned up the sea casting small fish to shore and toppling corals. *I can't just stand there and let the little fish flit about until they are caught unawares. Oh, what can I do?*

Helpless to Help

I wanted to warn those fish. I shouted, not caring about the stares of people on shore, "Friends, little fish and crabs and squishy old Mr. octopus. Please dive deep into the bay and hide in the caves by the big rock. You will be safe from the hurricane that's coming."

The butterfly fish darted past my feet. Crabs crawled over the small rocks on the sea bottom. A school of sailfin tangs swished by. They paid no attention to me.

I screamed in frustration. "Go hide deep in the sea. A storm is coming." But it was no use. Not one creature tried to find a safe place to hide. They didn't even know I stood there shouting. They couldn't see the black wall coming closer and closer.

I wish I had my SCUBA gear on, I thought. *I'd strap on my air tank, pull on my dive fins, and wrap my weight belt around my waist. I'd hurry because the storm is blowing nearer. I'd jump into the beautiful bay where the water is still so calm and the fish flit about in shallow water.*

Then I realized, of course, that I could not warn them at all. I did not know fish language, not one word of it. I saw the danger, but had no way of telling my tiny friends. Even if I waved my arms and kicked my fins at them to scare them into a cave, they would only stay a moment until I swam off to another part of the bay to scare other fish. Then they'd all dart out to play in the calm, clear water and search for food. Not one fish saw the danger, and no matter how wild I could thrash about, the fish would soon ignore me. I felt hopeless.

A whole world separated me from the fish I loved. I was a land creature. A human. And I could only visit their world and watch. They thrived in their watery home. I realized, with a sudden jolt, that the only way to help them would be to become one of them. I'd have to sprout fins, grow a tail, develop gills, and learn to dart among the corals. I'd have to learn fish language, swim in schools with other fish, and slither into coral crevices like the shy wrasses. I'd even have to wiggle beneath the sand with the flounders. Only then, would they listen. I'd tell them I loved them, do kind things for them so they'd believe me, and then guide them to deep places for safety.

But becoming a fish would take a miracle. Becoming a fish would be dangerous. A shark might catch me and tear me to pieces, or a tiger moray eel slash me with its needle-like teeth. Becoming a fish could cost me my life.

I sighed, removed my fins and sloshed toward shore. "Dear God, you made those fish. Please look after them. Thanks," I prayed.

So *That's* How God Felt

Later that day I sat curled up in my warm bungalow as the rain pounded the window and the wind whirled through the palm trees. I thought about my tiny friends in the cold, churning water.

"That's it, I shouted, jumping to my feet. "That's just the way You felt when you saw the storm of sin heading for Your world. A world full of beautiful people that you created! Oh, it must have been terrible. No wonder you came. You knew sin would kill every person who lived here if You didn't do something to help.

I felt that I had just looked into God's heart for a wonderful second. He was out there. He had stood up in far away Heaven, looked down at the storm-tossed world, and felt the pain. The One who created us and loved us became one of us so He could be here and speak our language. He healed the sick, spoke kindly to the sad, taught the ignorant, held the children. Then when He won our trust, He showed us a way to hide in His love through the storms and promised us a forever life with Him.

I remembered the verse in John 1:14: "So the Word of God [Jesus] became a man and lived among us. We saw that Light with our own eyes and knew He was from God. Jesus was gracious, kind and full of light and truth." The thought made me jump up and down inside.

Now trace the way God uses an adventure like this to increase *your* love for Him. Did you get drawn into the story, visualizing yourself slithering through the water? Did you feel some of the joy of discovery? How did you feel about the possible destruction of the fish? Could you imagine yourself trying to find a way to save them? What did you learn about your Creator and His plan to save you? What do you think will happen to you the next time you see a school of fish flitting around in a tank, an aquarium, or in the actual ocean? Could you come up with a Bible verse of your own that fits the truth demonstrated by the adventure?

I challenge you to start a notebook, right now, in which you can jot down your own adventures and what you learn from them.

Because you have discovered treasures in nature that help you know your Creator, you will choose to open His Word and search for more.

CHAPTER SIX

Listening to the Heart Mender

God is there, but we can't see Him. Our eyes are on other things.

MARY FEASTS ON HIS WORDS

"The people follow Him everywhere," Martha said. "He hardly has time to eat. I can't remember the last time He's had a full night's sleep." She looked up from the robe she was mending with a frown. This time of day little light came through the narrow window in their main room, and she found it hard to see.

"I know," Mary nodded. "I worry about Him too. But can you blame the people? For their whole lives all they've heard is the arguing between the priests and scribes. Beyond that, they've hardly ever gotten anything from them but condemnation."

"The Teacher's words are certainly different." Martha laughed, thinking of the story Jesus told about the wise man who built his house upon a rock instead of the sand.

"He has compassion for people," Mary said after thinking a moment. "No matter how many crowd Him or line up to see him, He's never impatient. He never pushes them away. Healing flows out of Him like rivers of life."

Martha nodded. "Yes, and even I can understand His simple, wonderful lessons. They pour over me like a soothing balm."

The women sat in companionable silence. Suddenly Mary asked, "Did you hear someone call?"

Martha put down her mending and opened the front door.

"Here!" their friend Deborah exclaimed, not waiting to be invited in. She thrust a triangle of flatbread and a piece of dried fish into Martha's hands, then pushed past her and gave Mary the same.

"Eat it," she commanded. "It's delicious. You'll see."

The sisters exchanged puzzled glances. Mary bit off a small piece of the bread. Martha placed the fish on her piece of bread and bit into both.

"Isn't it wonderful!" Deborah said. "I saved you both some. Jesus made it."

"Sit down, Deborah," Martha said with a laugh, pointing to a tapestry on the floor near the window. "What is this is about? What do you mean, 'Jesus made it'?"

Deborah was too excited to sit. She paced the room, gesturing with her hands. "I was there! I saw the whole thing with my own eyes. I could hardly believe it, but, it's true."

"The bread is good and the fish very tasty," Mary said, "But you must tell us why you brought this to us. You know we have plenty of food."

"But you don't have *miracle* bread and fish," Deborah objected. "Yesterday I joined a crowd of people who followed Jesus around to the other side of the Sea of Galilee. You know how Jerusalem is just packed with people because of the Passover. They come from all over," she added unnecessarily. "Well, Jesus got into a boat and headed out across the lake. I don't know if He wanted to get away or what, but everyone followed. People jumped into boats and others—like me—just walked around the shore til we found Him on the other side."

"Deborah," Mary said, "that's a long ways to walk."

"Don't I know it!" she agreed. "But it was worth every blister. And the further we walked the more people joined us."

Martha had taken up her sewing again, and now bent down to bite off a thread. "I'm glad you went," she told her friend. "I'd have walked all that way, too, if I'd been there, and I want to hear what Jesus talked about. But first, what's all this excitement about the bread?"

Miracle Bread

"Oh, Martha!" Deborah breathed. "I wish you both had been there. Everyone wanted to hear Him, of course. No one speaks as He does! He taught us all day. He said, 'I am the Water of Life. I am the Bread of Heaven.' And then He explained these symbols in such a way that even the children—you know how the children always want to be right on top of Him—could understand it. It was wonderful." Deborah lifted her hands then crossed her arms over her heart. There was no real way to explain it, to truly express the way Jesus had taught them and how it touched her heart. Tears filled her eyes.

"No one wanted to leave Him, girls. It was getting late, but no one left. He'd sort of finished talking—He seemed tired—and was playing with the children." Her face softened. "You should have seen Him. I know didn't want to leave, but I'd gotten so empty, and the sun was pretty low."

"Deborah, you stayed too late!" Martha objected.

"Don't be hard on me," Deborah said. "Someone said that a lot of the people there had been with Him for three days. They forgot about eating, and they'd just slept on the grass."

"How strange," Martha murmured.

"What about the bread?" Mary asked.

"*He* made it," Deborah told them. "His disciples wanted to send us away into the villages to buy food, but Jesus took charge. He told everyone to sit down on the grass in groups." She shook her head. "There were 5,000 people there, 5,000 men. Of course, as many women—maybe more—and children. So we're sitting in these groups and Jesus took five barley loaves and two small fish from a boy's lunch. He held them up toward heaven and prayed."

"What did He say?" Mary asked, hanging on every word.

"It's amazing how His voice carries, you know." A smile lit her whole face. "So he held up this little lunch and thanked God for always hearing Him, and He asked for a blessing on the food. That's all. Then He broke the loaves and the fishes into pieces and dropped them into a basket. When the first basket was full one of the disciples picked it up and started passing it to the crowd. Jesus kept on breaking the bread and the fish, dropping it into the next basket. He kept on until 12 baskets had been filled and passed through this mob! We ate all we wanted. Jesus let us take the extra bread and fish home to share."

"Are you telling me that I just ate bread that Jesus made with His own hands . . . out of a little boy's lunch?" Mary's eyes grew big and her hand flew up to her mouth.

"That's just what I've been trying to tell you."

"Is there anything Jesus can't do?" Martha asked, more to herself than the others. She shook her head in amazement. "This proves, again, that He cares about people's physical as well as their spiritual needs.

"And He made it happen with just a few words," Deborah exclaimed. "His words are powerful. They nourish my heart and my soul. Oh, Mary, I'm so glad you told me about Him," she cried, flinging herself into Mary's arms. Martha joined them and the three clung to each other, laughing with the joy that their friend Jesus had brought into their lives.

I wish I could have been there with Deborah. Not just to taste the bread, but to listen to the powerful words of Jesus. I know you wish you could have heard them, too. The wonderful truth is that we can hear His words and benefit from their power today, for Jesus left us with the written word. His followers through the ages have recorded, under the direction of the Holy Spirit, the words He wanted us to have. You can read the story of how Jesus fed the 5,000 in Matthew 14:13-21, in Mark 6:32-44, in Luke 9:10-17, and again in John 6:1-13. Every time you read it, your faith will be nourished.

To feel the real power of God's promises, repeat them out loud.

I Discover the Power of His Words

"I'll be back by 12:00 so we can go shelling," I yelled at Thelma as George eased the dive boat from the shallow water and headed out toward the reef.

"Don't worry," George called to Thelma. "We'll be back in time for you girls to go out on the sand bar at low tide."

Whew, I thought. *In the morning I dive with George, and then I have to keep up with Thelma as she moves along the sand bars like a sanderling.* I didn't have more time to think about the busy day ahead because George stopped the boat near the reef and tossed the anchor overboard. We suited up, and I jumped off the back of the boat and was swallowed by the cool water. I sank to the sand and waited for my dive buddy to join me on the bottom of the sea.

Just as soon as George reached the bottom he gave me the OK signal, then turned and headed off across the sandy lagoon toward the reef. George didn't stop to poke around looking for shells. He cruised along the reef, pumping his big fins. I followed, making my small pink fins go as fast as I could. He slithered through a narrow cave. I followed. He rose up over the top of the reef and down the other side. I followed, stopping only long enough to peer into a basket sponge. Then I spotted some small rocks scattered along the edge of the reef. I wanted to turn over every one of those rocks to see what kind of creatures were living under them. I was tired of cruising. I felt tired of following George around. Suddenly he stopped to stare at a grouper, and I had my chance. I didn't stop. I just kept swimming straight ahead. Straight for those rocks.

Now George had to follow me. He just lay in the water watching me turn over the rocks. But when I picked up a blue sea star and held it up for him to see, he decided to turn some rocks over too. We found scallops and crabs and held them up for the other to see.

After awhile we found ourselves in a great sandy field called a sea lagoon. I knew no shells would dare to walk around out there in the open. I knew that God wrote a message in each shells brain that says "stay hidden during the day. Hide in a cave. Crawl under a rock. Slither into a crack in the reef. Stay hidden." I knew that every sea creature knew the message and followed the message. That's how they stayed safe.

I signaled George that I wanted to return to the reef. We had just started to turn around and head back for the reef when we saw something amazing. There on the white sand sat the biggest Florida horse conch I'd ever seen. I headed right toward it. Then I noticed that it was connected to a big pink queen conch. George and I hovered over the two big shells. We both shrugged our shoulders as if to say, "I don't know what they are doing, but they are in danger out here in the open." The shells twisted and turned in the sand. Sand particles floated up in the water.

"They are fighting!" I wanted to tell George, but couldn't talk without losing my air supply. Both of them have forgotten the message God wrote inside their brain, and they both came out from their hiding places. They thought they were strong. They thought they could ignore the warning messages in their brains. They got busy fighting. They forgot all about the danger around them from enemies larger than themselves. We both stared at the foolish shells who held each other in a death grip, each trying to eat the other.

We realized that they'd only destroy one another or be killed by a passing enemy, so we decided to try to take them to the boat. George motioned for me to grab the great horse conch. He clutched the other. We both pulled and pulled. Suddenly the two shells came apart. George and I both fell backward onto the sand. It didn't feel very good because lying on a round metal air tank is not comfortable.

I struggled to turn over and, still grasping the horse conch. I looked at George. He held the pink queen conch in his hands. Neither creature seemed to be alive. Parts of both their bodies were missing.

George gave me the thumbs up sign to signal that he wanted to go up to the boat. We rose slowly in the water, both clutching our shells. We climbed into the boat and looked at our prizes.

"My horse conch is 22 inches long. The longest horse conch on record is only one inch longer," I told him. "It's a prize."

"And this is a mighty big conch, too," George said. "Too bad these creatures aren't still down in the reef."

"If only they'd listened to the message written in their brains and stayed under cover, we wouldn't have found them half dead like this," I said.

The Heart Mender

You and I aren't born with instinct written in our brain as are animals and God's sea creatures, but we do have the written word. God tells us, "I will put my laws in their minds and write them on their hearts. I will be their God, and they will be my people" (Jeremiah 31:33).

Don't wait to find time to study God's words. Don't struggle to squeeze a place into your schedule for moments with Him. Make it first! Put your connection with Jesus first, and God will help you complete your other tasks. God's powerful words in your heart will nourish your soul in the same way that His bread filled the hunger of those who sat at His feet 2,000 years ago.

The important thing is make the choice without waiting for the desire. As you read the Bible the Holy Spirit will increase your desire until it becomes the most natural thing in the world for you to do.

Listen to what David, God's friend, decided:

"The one thing I ask of the Lord, the thing I look for is to remain close to Him my entire life, to see the beauty of His character and to talk with Him in His Temple" (Psalm 27:4).

Jesus is like a treasure. You discover Him, you choose Him, and then you go on choosing to know Him better day by day. Of course, that makes Satan angry for he is working to crowd Jesus out of your life. I learned an important lesson about this from an abalone shell.

The One I Lost

I climbed down the rocks piled along the edge of California's Monterey Bay. Sparkling water lapped against its half moon edges, and houses nestled themselves among the bumpy hillsides just beyond.

I felt the urge to slosh among the tide pools cupped by the rocks and search for treasure, but the November water looked cold and the wind that blew through my hair scattered goose bumps across my skin.

Suddenly I got an idea. I raised my field glasses to my eyes and scanned the clear water. I spotted a tiny abalone shell caught among the rocks and climbed down the cliff, snatching it just before a small wave could catch me.

Hey, this is the way to shell on a wintery day, I thought happily.

Finally I got tired and sat down to rest and enjoy watching the fat brown sea lions slung like old rags over the rocky breakwater.

Out of the corner of my eye I spotted a sea otter gliding along on his back. He flipped his finned feet and floated into the harbor. Closer and closer he came. I could see that he held a huge abalone shell on his stomach. He took a bite from its contents, washed his whiskers with two front paws, and stuffed another bite into his mouth. Then he rolled over in the water, using the sea like a napkin to remove stray bits of abalone from his hairy chest. Every second brought him closer to my spot on the rocks.

I held by breath as he glided to within 10 feet of my perch. He paused, rolled over, and came up licking the now empty shell. I really got excited, but hardly dared to move lest he spot me and speed away. When he turned over again and came up without the shell I scanned the sandy bottom with my binoculars. I could see that abalone not more than 20 feet away. It glistened like an underwater rainbow. The kid in me began to jump up and down.

I pulled off my sweat shirt, pushed up my shirt sleeves, and plunged in. That cold water enveloped me and I gasped, but I kept my eyes on the shell. November's wind clutched at my wet clothes, but I kept moving toward my prize. "Help me reach it," I prayed "I just have to get the abalone that sea otter brought right to me. Please, please let me get it."

The water surged back and forth threatening to push me over, but I kept my eyes on that shiny abalone. Deeper and deeper the water grew until it reached my armpits. I wished I'd brought my mask and snorkel, but I never dreamed I'd get into that frigid water.

With the water up to my shoulders, I touched the shell with a sneaker-clad foot and gave it a little kick toward shore. A swell caught me and nearly knocked me down, but I kept nudging the shell toward the rocky edge. It took a long time to work it close to shore into the shallow water.

At last I thought I could pick it up, but as I bent over, the water caught my face. "Brr!" I shouted. I'd have to get it into shallower water. *I just can't stand to get my face and hair wet,* I thought.

I gave that abalone one last shove, and it disappeared from sight.

"Oh, no" I cried, staring into the crevices among the rocks. I couldn't see the abalone anymore.

My legs begged me to give up and put on something warm and dry, but how I hated to give up the search. At last the cold forced me from the water. People stared at me as I dripped and shivered along the road toward the car, but I didn't care. My only thought was of ways I could recapture my prize.

Rummaging around in the car trunk until I found my inflatable view box, I ran back to the water's edge and waded in. Ten feet off the rocky edge I began to search anew. I could see the bottom clearly but no matter how hard I tried to locate it, I couldn't see my lost prize. And up in heaven, no one answered my cries for help. At last, shaking from the cold, I decided to give it up. I felt awful. Tears spilled down my cheeks.

Why didn't you help me find that abalone? I questioned God. *I know you sent that sea otter along, but why couldn't you help me get it to shore?* Then I realized that maybe God had a lesson for me.

When you and I come into the harbor of His love, when we discover Him like a treasure, we are filled with joy. His acceptance, forgiveness, and kindness are like the colors of the beautiful abalone shell. But it is so easy to lose Him in the frantic pace of our lives. He's there, but we can't see Him because our eyes are on other things. We forget our need of His presence, and we carelessly let Him drop out of sight, just as I did the abalone shell.

Somewhere on a rocky harbor edge hides a beautiful abalone shell that will never be seen again. Winter storms will bash it against the rocks and break it to pieces. It's lost, and I'm sad. Sometimes I think about how different it could have been if I'd just risked getting my face wet and grabbed it when it sat there so close to me. I would have it right now to show you. Instead, my hands are empty. I lost the treasure through carelessness. I failed to make it the number one priority at the moment. And you will find that if you go many days without taking in the treasure of God's words, your heart will be empty. Not only that, you will find that your old fears and temptations will wash over you when your grasp on Jesus is weak.

Swallowed by a Wave

I stood on a bluff gazing out over the green Pacific Ocean. Great waves crashed against the rocks below me and swirled into the curve of the narrow beach that hugged the rock wall. Lupine and California poppies grew in swirls of blue and gold right up to the edge of the rocky cliffs.

"This is the spot," I said to my kids, Sally, Steve, and David. "We can set up our picnic on the small beach down there," I told them, pointing to a band of white sand.

Sally peered over the cliff. "How will we get down there," she asked.

"There's a path somewhere," I said, searching through the tall grass.

"Here it is," I cried over the sound of the surf. "Let's go."

We made our way carefully along the path that wound itself down the cliff. The instant we reached the end of the trail, I sat down kicking off my shoes and digging my feet into the warm sand. I noticed that a dozen others had also found this secluded spot along Laguna's ragged coast.

The water seemed to call me. "Come on and dive in," it said. I jumped up and headed for the water.

"Get the lunch out," I yelled to the kids. "I'll be right back."

I splashed my way toward the deep water and plunged in. When I came up for air I noticed that the waves beyond looked big. They looked bigger than any waves I'd ever seen before. A sudden prickly feeling swept over me, but I kept swimming. My hands clawed at the water, moving me closer and closer toward the breakers. Then I burst through the surface and stood up. "Wow!" I cried.

A great wall of water rose up before me. It hovered above me like a helicopter, the wind catching its wig of foam and splattering it into my face.

Dive quick! Dive deep! my mind commanded, remembering that the water beneath a wave is calm.

I hesitated for an instant. The wall of water leaned forward and tumbled toward me, rushing like a wild animal to the spot where I stood. At last I leaped into action. I dove!

You're too late, an inner voice wailed as the wave swallowed me up. It poured itself into my lungs and rubbed sand into my hair. Then spit me out in water near the beach.

I gulped air and stumbled to my feet. The water tugged at my legs as it ran back down the slope of the beach to join the sea behind me. I stared at the dry land just a few feet beyond my reach. Men laughed as they threw Frisbees back and forth. Children giggled and patted the wet sides of sand castles. Women hid behind magazine covers. They did not see my desperate struggle.

I begged my feet to take me to the safe shore, but they refused to move.

Then I felt it. Water thundered against the sand behind me like a giant train charging down a railroad track. *Run, run, run,* my brain screamed, but my legs refused to budge. They buckled, and I crumpled into the smashing surf.

That wave grabbed me and rolled me around and around like a wet towel in a clothes dryer. It thumped my face against the sea bottom like a boy pounds a basketball across the court. It flipped me over onto my back like a pancake and tore all the air out of my lungs. Then it shook me out into shallow water. This time I couldn't even stand up.

"Need help?" a voice called from the shore.

I wiped the sand and water from my eyes and noticed a man running along the wet sand. He wore blue swim trunks and a baseball cap. He grabbed the cap and waved it at me. "Hold on, the lifeguard's coming," he shouted.

Hope sprang into my heart. *Help!* I wanted to scream. *I'm in big trouble.* But, for one foolish moment, I hesitated.

I looked at the cluster of people gathering on the dry sand. They had just watched the bronzed lifeguard jump from his tower, grab the red life raft, and dash down the beach. They had craned their necks and peered through sunglasses to see him swim toward me.

Wait a minute, I thought. *I'm a SCUBA diver. I've dived into half the seas around the world. I don't need help. The shore is so close. I have to show these people that I . . .*

Then I heard it. Another wave roaring toward the very place

where I lay like a heap of seaweed. This time I didn't hesitate. "Help!" I sputtered. I looked through bleary eyes. The lifeguard was almost there. He grabbed me up in his strong arms and carried me to shore.

The crowd clapped! They clapped because the lifeguard had done his job. They clapped because I had sense enough to let him save me.

Soon I huddled within the cocoon of a warm blanket far from the reach of the waves. In just a few minutes I'd discovered how helpless I could be, how good the strong grasp of the lifeguard felt, and the great joy of planting my feet on dry land.

Just as the words "the lifeguard is coming" put hope into my heart, the words of Jesus have the power to banish fear and help you reach up and receive the help He brings. But since it is not natural to reach for the Word, you will need to do it from intelligent choice. You will need to set aside a special time of day to feast on His messages. Once you decide upon a time and a place, let others know of your decision so they will respect this time. Each time you stop to listen, the habit will become stronger and your hunger greater.

This time I didn't hesitate. "Help," I sputtered.
The crowd clapped—because I
had sense enough to let him save me.

How to Discover Jesus in the Word

1. LOOK FOR WORDS THAT PAINT PICTURES OF HIS CHARACTER

One of the best ways to benefit from and enjoy God's word is to ask yourself questions as you read: What picture of Jesus do I see in this verse? What is God trying to show me about Himself? In this way you will "see" Him, and as you look at Him this way, you will change.

The Heart Mender

Some Bible verses actually paint a picture for you. Look at this verse as an example.

" 'He will be a sanctuary in time of need to those who trust Him. However, He will be a stumbling block to the unbelieving of Israel, like a rock that makes them fall. To the people of Jerusalem He will be a trap, where their sin of not trusting Him will be exposed' " (Isaiah 8:14).

Pick out the objects mentioned in this verse that tell you what Jesus is like. First, He's like a sanctuary. Imagine Jesus as a safe place, a refuge or a comfortable spot. The more you learn about the word the author has chosen to use, the more detail your picture will have. I understand the word "sanctuary" better since I learned that the Jews built cities of sanctuary—sometimes called cities of refuge—for those who needed a safe place to run when accused of crimes. They could stay in these sanctuary cities until their case could be heard. Jesus is a city of sanctuary for us. We can run to Him and be at peace.

Look at the word rock. What a picture! God wants so badly for all to be saved that he is willing to block the path of sinners, to make them fall so they will stop and recognize the troubled path they are taking. Then as if to emphasize this truth, Jesus says that He is like a trap, catching a wayward sinner. He will do anything to keep someone from destruction. He wants you to imagine yourself, slipping and sliding on a steep pathway that leads downward. You sin again and again. You may not even realize it, but the fact is that all sin leads down toward death. No one knows this better than Jesus, so He blocks the way down. What love! He puts Himself in front of you as you travel down the wrong road. You will have to pass right over Him or work your way around Him. You'll have to trip over Him. The One who loves you doesn't want you to be hurt by sin, nor to go on sinning even more and suffer greater hurt.

Isaiah paints pictures that bring the character of your Heart Mender to life with emotion, color, and sound.

Even the simplest verse holds a picture of some kind. Look at this one:

> "Previously, Jesus had been invited to the house of a
> Pharisee named Simon, whom He had healed of
> leprosy" (Matt. 26:6).

Ask yourself, What picture of Jesus do I see in this verse? What is God trying to show me about Himself?

You can discover a lot in just this one sentence. First, Jesus was sociable. He visited in people's homes, and people liked to have him. He had been invited to Simon's house. This verse also tells you that He had the power to cleanse a leper with a word. Imagine Him healing someone with cancer or AIDS with a word.

Now read Isaiah 10:14:

> " 'As simply as one reaches into a nest, so I reached out
> and took the wealth of nations. As easily as men
> collect eggs,
> I collected whole countries. Not one country
> flapped its wings at me
> to scare me away or opened its beak to scream at me.' "

If you've actually collected eggs from an angry hen this verse will come alive for you. But if you haven't, just use your imagination. Can't you just see that hen flapping its wings in resistance when you attempt to gather her eggs! Of course this wouldn't prevent you from taking the eggs because you're smarter and stronger than the chicken. In this verse Jesus is saying that no one can resist what He wants to do. God is in control.

Now if you want to really understand this verse, go into a hen house and experience it for yourself. You will have an adventure and come to know for yourself what God is trying to say to you.

As you add picture after picture to your album you will be drawn closer and closer to Him until sin completely loses its hold. That's why Satan will do anything to keep you from looking at Christ. John understood this principle for when he saw Jesus coming toward him John cried out to the people who'd come to hear him, " 'Behold, the Lamb of God, who will take away the sins of the world!' " (John 1:29).

2. SEARCH FOR INSTRUCTION

God's Word is full of helpful instruction. Just as the physician hands you an information sheet to guide you in preparing for surgery, God provides instructions that help you walk with Him. Watch for these as you read.

Take a look at Isaiah 34:1.

> "Come and listen, all you nations of earth.
>   Come and pay attention, all you people.
>   Let the earth and everyone in it hear
>   what the Lord has to say."

Look for the verbs. They tell you what actions you should take. Let's list them: Come, listen, pay attention, and he will tell you exactly what to do.

3. WATCH FOR WARNINGS

In Isaiah 46, God gives instructions and encouragement. Then He adds these words (verse 8) as if to alert you to your great need:

> "'Remember what I just said and take it to heart.
>   Fix it in your minds so you won't forget it.'"

Now let's look at the picture Isaiah paints to show us how foolish it is to go to the wrong person for advice. It's found in Isaiah 47:13-15:

> "'You're powerless in spite of all the advice you get from your astrologers and stargazers who map out the heavens and make their monthly predictions. Let them save you from what is coming. Their advice is like straw thrown on a fire. They can't even save themselves. The fire that will sweep through the land will not be a fire that you sit by to warm yourself. You've consulted these astrologers all your life, but what good will they be to you?'"

4. Discover and believe His promises

God appears sad in this verse, Isaiah 48:18.

> "'If you had only listened to me and paid attention to what I told you, your peace would have been like the gentle flow of still waters and your righteousness as powerful as the waves of the sea.'"

The people of Israel failed to choose Jesus as their Savior. You can see the terrible results. But it can be different with you. Reverse your actions. Choose to listen and obey, and you will have that special peace and the powerful covering of His righteousness. Reading God's word is like taking living seeds inside yourself. Each idea, like a seed, takes root and brings a harvest of faith and trust.

Every word is backed up by a living God who says that "'those who put their hope in me and wait for my help will not be disappointed'" (Isaiah 49:23).

5. Memorize His words

Advertisers know the principle of repetition. They understand how a catchy song, repeated over and over, will bring the image of a product into your mind and induce you to purchase that object. They have simply discovered one of God's principles. Memorizing God's word and singing it, furnishes you with a storehouse of hopeful messages that will come into your mind when you need them most.

If you want to feel the real power of God's promises, repeat them out loud. Then say, "I believe your words, Lord. I choose to trust You and to accept Your will for me."

Your mind hears these words, and this helps build hope and endurance. It also pushes away the negative words of the tempter. I am sure of this because of the words recorded in James 4:7: "Submit to God. Resist the devil, and he will flee from you."

6. Establish power formulas

Since God's words are real, alive and powerful, you can expect them to produce results in your life. I find it helpful to make formulas that help me see cause and effect. A formula is made up of ingredients placed together to bring about a certain result. God often tells you what is needed to produce a desired result. Take a look at this example we find in 1 John 4:16-18.

> "We know and rely on the love God has for us because God is love. And anyone who lives out this love lives in God and God in him. We know that our love is being perfected when we can look forward to the Day of Judgment with confidence and live a life of love like Christ did in a world of sin. Fear and love just don't go together. Love dispels fear because fear focuses on punishment and won't let love mature. The one who is afraid of God does not understand God's love."

These verses clearly explain how love, perfected by experience, pushes fear and anxiety away. They also tell how to grow the kind of love that destroys fear. Pick out the action wards that tell you what you must do to obtain a desired result. In this case, the desire is for a sense of fearlessness. Personalize these actions by using the word *I*.

What I do? I know God's love. (I gather information and learn about His love.)

I believe God's love. (I choose to believe. I adopt God's love as a reality.)

I live a loving life. (I practice being loving. I continue to live or abide in His love.)

Results of this kind of perfected love:
* can't go together with fear
* destroys fear
* dispels fear

When put into a formula that shows what I must do and what the outcome will be, it looks like this:

I know God's love + I believe God's love + I abide in God's love = fearlessness

Now consider this formula and make a choice to believe it. God's power will give you the desired gift, a fearless heart.

Formulas help you "see" how God goes about changing your life. They help you "see" how to cooperate with your Heart Mender.

Now that you are soaking up the powerful, true words of Jesus, you will want to talk with Him.

CHAPTER SEVEN

Talking With the Heart Mender

I visualize myself curled up on His lap.

MEETING JESUS

 Imagine that you lie on your sleeping mat staring into the darkness. Yesterday the doctor told you that you have less than six months to live. There is no cure for your illness, but there might be a ray of hope.

You heard someone say that Jesus was seen crossing Galilee into Phoenicia. He might pass nearby as your home is just outside town. Since He has healed even lepers, you ponder, perhaps He will heal you. You decide to slip away before your family awakens, so you get up, wrap your cloak around you, and tiptoe to the front door. You open it slowly and quietly. Once out in the crisp air, you hurry down the path.

According to Jewish thought, you are a heathen, a Gentile. You ask yourself, *Will Jesus take notice of my trouble?*

The sun is rising as you see a small group of men and women coming through the town gate. They are clustered around a man who is talking with them as they walk. You hurry to join them and know, in an instant, that the man is Jesus. You wonder, fearful, *Dare I ask for His help?*

"Hello," a woman greets you, leaving Jesus' side and walking back to where you follow at a distance. She motions for you to come closer. "I'm Mary. Do you want to speak to Jesus?"

"Yes," you stammer. "I have heard of Him. Everyone says He is so kind. He heals all those who come to Him. Is this true?

"Oh, yes," Mary says. "Oh, yes!"

"Lord, help me. Have mercy on me," a voice cries. You and Mary whirl around to see a woman running down the path toward you. Her bare feet kick up a small cloud of dust, and the wind catches her red and gold robe. Suddenly she trips, falling on the stony path. Immediately she leaps to her feet, running faster than before. As soon as she gets near, she begins to call out again, "Have mercy on me, O Lord. Have mercy on me."

Jesus continues walking and teaching, ignoring her cries until one of His disciples interrupts. "Master. Send her away. She's annoying us."

You see a sad look cross Jesus' face, but He goes on speaking as if nothing occurred.

The woman does not give up. Running, stumbling, she pushes past the disciples until she is next to Jesus. "Lord, my daughter is grievously vexed with a devil. Please help me," she cries, looking into His face.

You watch, holding your breath. Now you will see for yourself what kind of man Jesus is. You will know if you should approach Him. You expect to see one of the miracles you've heard so much about, but instead, Jesus acts disinterested. "My commitment is to help the Israelites," He says, looking at the woman then continuing on His way.

Desperate, the woman sprints ahead of Jesus, falling at His feet. "Please help me," she cries.

He stops. The crowd stops. Every eye is fastened on His face. "It's not right to take the family dinner and give it to the dogs," He says quietly.

You gasp. You look at Mary. She seems as surprised as you are.

The woman bows her head. "That's true, Lord," she agrees. "But family dogs are taken care of by their owners and are given the leftovers."

Then you see Jesus smile. He reaches out, saying, "I really do care about you and your daughter. Your request is granted. Your daughter is now well."

The woman remains on the ground, weeping. The group walks on. You can't move. Long moments pass, then the woman stands up, gathers her robe about herself, and strides toward town. To your surprise, she is singing. You stare at her retreating form, then turn to follow the group, but you feel troubled.

Later you seek out Mary among the group sitting around a small fire. She nods as you sit down. Jesus is still teaching, but you hardly hear Him. You're troubled by the question, Why was this famous Teacher so unkind to this woman?

Getting up from your place by the fire, you walk to a nearby olive tree. Leaning on its gnarled trunk, you turn the problem over and over in your mind.

"What's the matter?" a woman asks. It is Mary.

"I don't understand why Jesus spoke to that mother in such a manner."

"I didn't either," Mary admits. "But now I understand. I think Jesus treated the woman the way we might have—cruel, not wanting to be bothered. He wanted us to see the ugliness of our attitude toward the Gentiles. He had every intention of helping her, and He did." Mary takes your hand. "Jesus often teaches by example. I'm glad the mother didn't give up. She had courage."

Suddenly you decide. You will trust Him, too. You will bring your trouble to Him, right now. "Jesus!" you cry. "Have mercy on *me*. I am ill." Now it's your turn to press through the group huddled about the Healer. "Help me!"

How to Come to Jesus With Your Needs
1. Stop!

The moment I opened my eyes, I grabbed the long list that sat on the night stand. "Better get at it," I sighed.

What about your worship? a voice whispered.

I pushed away the thought and reached for the paper towels. "Windows first," I said to myself.

Jesus always spent time with God before He started His work, the voice continued. I plunked into a chair. "It's true," I sighed. "He went out into nature. He sang. He prayed. Maybe that's why He had so much power and joy in His life."

Suddenly my plan to attack spring cleaning at 5:00 a.m. didn't seem important. I threw the towels onto the counter, grabbed my back pack, and headed for the beach.

I carved out a round place in the side of the sand dune, lay back against it, and waited for the sun to rise. A glimmer of gold spread itself across the sky. Then the sun burst over the horizon with a shout of reds and yellows. Its warm fingers touched the cold dunes and nudged the tiny ghost crabs that hid in deep holes along the shore line.

I lay still and stared at a nearby small hole. Soon a tiny claw appeared followed by a round hairy body. Two eyes perched on long stalks whirled around in opposite directions. I held my hand over my mouth to push back the laughter. The crab caught my movement and froze. Then thinking I was just a piece of driftwood slung against the sand dune by the sea, the crab ventured out.

First it paused, allowing the warm sun to dance all over its little body. I knew it felt good because the sun touched me, too.

Next the ghost crab searched the sky for gulls. Seeing only clouds, it scampered sideways down the slope of sand toward the sea where it dipped thirsty gills into the water. After searching the sky once more, it raced back to its hole and disappeared.

How smart, I thought. When the crab awoke it could have said, "I'd better get busy. My house needs a good airing so I'll have to remove the roof. The living room is just too small. I think I'll dig it out a bit." It could have decided to scurry over and have a claw to claw talk with the neighbor. But, no. It basked in the sun, then ran to the sea.

"The creature is imitating its Creator," I whispered. I decided that every morning as the sun eased itself over the horizon, I'd copy the crab who showed me a picture described in Mark 1:35: "Then early the next morning, a long time before daybreak, Jesus . . . went up into the hills to a secluded place to talk with His Father."

Jesus went out because He wanted to let His heart rise up in praise to God. He wanted to read God's words and talk with Him. This became His plan of action, and I'd make it mine. Like Him, I'd linger in the warmth of the Sun of Righteousness and drink deeply of the Water of Life. Only then would I pick up my list.

I learned from a hairy crab that the first step in developing a dynamic prayer life is to STOP. The amazing thing is that you and I—women with mended hearts who desperately need God's power in our hearts—often plunge right into our day without prayer. This isn't intentional, but it's very foolish.

When I get up, my feet hit the floor running, so rule Number 1 is very important. I simply must STOP and remember to make contact with my God number one on my to-do list. Every time I make this choice the desire to continue strengthens. So don't go by your feelings or your schedule. Stop and take time for Him before you do anything else. You will find that your projects for the day will have His blessing.

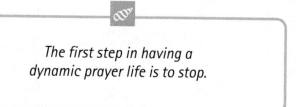

*The first step in having a
dynamic prayer life is to stop.*

2. Linger

This is the most difficult rule for you to adopt and follow. Lingering is almost a lost art in our fast-forward world. But learn to do it. Take time to connect with God. He is more than willing, in spite of His busy schedule, to linger with you. Lingering—rather than dashing through your devotions—brings tremendous joys you cannot experience any other way. Work time into your day, in spite of every demand, to linger with God. Savor the reality of His love, soak up His power. Linger long enough to let His joy fill your heart. This is the only way you will live above the fear, weakness, and troubles of life. There is no shortcut. None.

Of course, anytime you snatch a moment to communicate with God or read even a few words, you nurture your connection with the Heart Mender.

3. Praise Him

While it is true that God listens to every prayer that descends to His throne, your desire is to truly grow closer to Him, to trust His love, and to become radiant. Praise is one of your best choices. Something wonderful happens when you praise Him. And He receives your gratitude with an open heart.

I used to start my prayers by pouring out my troubles, but not anymore. First I thank Him for every blessing I can think of. On some days, this is not so easy because the difficulties loom larger than the solutions. But there is never a moment when I can't find concrete reasons to praise Him. Here are some suggestions that might help you unlock your heart and pour out praises.

* Praise Him for being the loving, caring and trustworthy God that He is.
* Thank Him for what He has done for you in the past. Be specific.
* Mention characteristics about Him that you appreciate such as kindness, forgiveness, creativity, faithfulness, and patience.
* Thank Him for past answers to prayers.
* Praise Him for beauties around you that bring you pleasure such as the sky, clouds, fish, flowers, raindrops, green grass, and birds soaring.
* Thank Him for His promises, and tell Him that you depend upon Him and are thankful that He will keep them.

4. Admit that You Need God

Come to God as a friend who knows everything about you and admit your need for His love, blessing, help, and power. Pride shouts, "I can do it myself." Submission is ready to admit need. When you are weak, then you will become strong. Sin is stronger than you. Since you want to be free of it, living a victorious life, admit that there isn't one thing you can do without His taking complete control.

Most women long for a soul mate who will understand their deepest feelings and who accept them as they are. They want someone to laugh with and who will join them in the adventures that mean the most to them. Jesus is that person and your relationship with Him is permanent, safe, and joyful. Admit it. You need Him.

5. Choose Forgiveness

"'I am willing to forgive you your sins because of who I am. I will blot out your transgressions and remember them no more'" (Isaiah 43:25).

Because God has offered you unlimited forgiveness and unconditional love, joy has burst inside you, making you radiant. Now, based on His gift to you, offer forgiveness to others. Forgiving them does not mean that what they did is not awful or unimportant. It means that you shift the responsibility of their act to God. Forgive yourself, too. Receive His forgiveness because it is freely offered.

Ask your Heart Mender to carry the feelings that will trouble you from time to time. When they emerge, give them to Him. This will save you from becoming a bitter person.

As a young pastor's wife, I remember coming in contact with several bitter women. I listened to their anger, saw their despair, and watched all joy fade from their hearts. In fact, they destroyed all joy that dared to crop up around them. I determined that if anything terrible happened to me, I would not become bitter. Of course when grief did come I had to choose day by day to lay everything at His feet. It was a constant choice. I believe I was spared a great deal of misery because of this choice. I can tell you from experience, He cares and He will carry you. Don't give in to earthly fears and hatred. Always remember, "'I have swept away your sins like a cloud; like a morning mist they are all gone. Come back to me, for I am the One who saved you'" (Isaiah 44:22).

6. Believe

Belief is a choice, a decision. Exercise your faith by choosing to believe regardless of your feelings at the moment. This faith is based upon the sure word of God, and like a muscle that is exercised, it will grow stronger. Choose a verse, read it and say, "I believe what you say, God. I choose to trust You."

One of my favorite verses is a simple one found in Isaiah 26:4: "'Trust in the Lord forever, for the Lord Jehovah is an eternal rock, the Rock of all ages.'"

When I read this verse I picture the great cliffs at the seaside. They have stood for as long as anyone can remember. I see myself like the abalone shells that cling to the smooth surface of the rocks. They look like a salad bowl, open on one side. The opening is filled with a large suction cup that can cling to rocks so well that the force of the waves smashing against them cannot remove them from their safe place. Sometimes abalone shells hide themselves in the crevice of rocks for additional safety.

After I visualize the verse I choose to believe. I say, "I believe You are my Rock. I choose You to be my safe hiding place."

7. Persevere

Keep asking. Don't give up just because your prayer is not answered immediately. God knows what He is doing, and He is doing something. His timing is as perfect as His love. Let Him know that you yield yourself to His direction and choices, knowing that no one else knows you better, nor loves you more. Cling to Him, reminding Him that He knows best and that you count on Him to answer you in the way that He knows is best.

8. Be Real

Open your heart to Jesus. Be honest. It is wonderful that He desires and encourages you to be yourself and share your true feelings, ideas, and desires. You can talk with Him at any time, in any place, and in whatever situation you find yourself. You cannot weary nor burden Him. The many difficulties that you face might confuse and worry you, but not Him. He has a thousand ways to solve your problems that you know nothing about. Be yourself.

9. Draw Near and Listen

Jesus says to you, "'Come close and listen to what I have to say. . . . If you had only listened to me and paid attention to what I told you, your peace would have been like the gentle flow of still waters and your righteousness as powerful as the waves of the sea,'" Isaiah 48:16-18.

I remember my prayer life right after my divorce. I spent a good deal of my time pouring out my woes, screaming in pain, and begging for help. At least I went to the right place to behave like this. God certainly accepted me as I was. But gently He led me to yield to His overpowering love. I started to listen to Him, because He had listened to me. My brother Grover helped me see that I could visualize myself curled up on His lap with my head resting on His shoulders. This idea fascinated me and troubled me. I had no idea God could relate to me in such a way. I discovered this verse: "'Those who put their hope in me and wait for my help will not be disappointed'" (Isaiah 49:23).

This verse means much to me as I continue to draw near Him. After being abandoned several times in my life by those who should have accepted, valued, and helped me, I have struggled to visualize a God who would not do the same. When things get tough I tend to say, "So He has left me, too."

But based on His character, it is impossible for this to be true. Now when Satan tempts me to pull away, I draw near to God. When I feel angry and let down, I draw near. When I feel hurt and afraid, I draw near. And when everything flows along just right, I still exercise the choice to come near and listen.

10. Pray With a Friend

Negative words, including unbelief, blame, anger and fearfulness can work havoc on the hearts and spirits of those who are dealing with their own struggles. Take care that you don't pour out the details of your concerns upon them. Instead, take all that to God who can carry it easily. But you can benefit from sharing your concerns with a friend and by listening to their concerns. Together you can approach God's throne. You can encourage each other to stay faithful to Jesus. Choose hopeful, trusting words when you speak with others.

Two Ways to Pray

My son David helped me realize the great power of positive words. Even though I was in the middle of a grief period he encouraged me to talk hope. I found that the effect of hopeful words is amazing. Look at these two approaches to sharing. In both situations, the speaker has good reason to be troubled and longs to seek support and encouragement.

Approach # 1

"I feel miserable. Nothing is going right. God never helps me. He has forsaken me. I can't stand it anymore. Why is He treating me like this?"

Approach # 2

"I'm hurting today and I'm struggling to remember how much He loves me. I am sure He does, because He doesn't lie. He says, 'I will never leave you nor forsake you.'"

At first glance, you might not see the great difference. First, both approaches let you know that the speaker is struggling. Second, both are reaching out. But the similarity ends there. The first speaker just dumps negative words and hopeless statements that burden and discourage, or even push away the person they've gone to for help. The second speaker admits troubled feelings, but reinforces verbally that they choose trust and desire encouragement.

Taught by a Brittle Star

I learned a great lesson about this very thing from some wiggly sea creatures called brittle stars.

I felt exhausted after a long SCUBA dive, so I paddled into shallow water to rest. Rainbow colored fish swished past, crabs scurried about, and lobsters twitched their antennas. I lingered, sloshing to and fro on the shimmering sea.

"I'm not going to search beneath one more rock nor peer into one more crevice," I said to the angel fish who darted past. "I am just going to lie here."

But small rocks strewn about the sand below begged me to turn them over. I couldn't stop thinking about the treasures that might hide beneath them. Finally I inhaled a gulp of air, dove, and flipped over a rock.

Three tiny, hairy creatures with stop sign-shaped bodies and long skinny arms stared up at me. "Brittle stars!" I shouted through my snorkel.

Each brittle star darted off in a different direction. One dropped into a hole, another pressed into a crevice in the coral, and the last scurried beneath a nearby rock. I laughed, then lifted the rock where the star had disappeared. He wiggled off for another rock. *This is fun,* I thought to myself and lifted that rock. This time the brittle star chose a giant rock to slide beneath. I couldn't lift the rock, so I surfaced and gulped in a new supply of air.

Forgetting all about my decision to rest, I dove down and moved a flat rock to see what might be hidden there. Six creatures hid beneath the rock. I recognized them as Amphodia Occidentalis, another variety of stars with thin smooth arms.

I choose one brittle star to chase and waited for it to dart off to a new hiding place.

Something amazing happened. Instead of darting off in different directions, looking for cover, they took each other by an arm or two and drew themselves into a tight mass. I stared at the mass of twitching arms, then removed my dive knife from its sheath strapped to my leg. I tried to push one star away from the others, but I couldn't separate the tangle of bodies. Finally I put the rock back into place and headed for the surface.

Later on shore, I searched for an explanation in one of my sea creature guides.

Scientists, the books told me, were determined to collect the brittle star Amphodia in spite of the difficulties. They tried lifting rocks and grabbing a specimen. These brittle stars did not scatter in all directions as other brittle stars commonly do. Instead, they tangled themselves together. Because brittle stars will drop their rays at the slightest touch, the scientists couldn't separate the stars without breaking them into pieces.

They decided to take liquid poison into the reef and pour it around the rocks where the brittle stars hid. This poison would drug the brittle stars so they couldn't twine together. So the rocks were lifted, the poison poured. Scientists waited a minute then reached for a specimen. But when the brittle stars sensed the poison, they joined arms, pressed together, and squeezed out a special chemical that absorbed the poison! It baffled the scientists who could only shake their heads in wonder.

Those scientists may have shrugged their shoulders and said, "What a mystery," but not me. Joy jumped up and down inside me. I said, "What a God!" He created Amphodia Occidentalis, the brittle star, to remind me that life is about sharing and pressing together. Their story helped me remember that I can take hold of others, encouraging and sharing in a positive, saving way just as Amphodia does beneath the sea.

Now that you have learned to connect to your Heart Mender through prayer, you will realize that you may receive a special gift.

CHAPTER EIGHT

The Gift of a Mended Heart

The Potter knows the person you long to be.

MARY'S JOYFUL HEART

"Mary!" Martha called as she walked across the back yard and into the vineyard. "Where are you?"

"I'm over here at the far end of the vines," Mary said, waving her arm so Martha could see her.

"Did you get the extra bread baked?" Mary asked.

"Yes, but I could have done it quicker had you stayed and helped another hour."

"I know, Martha," Mary said, looking up from the cluster of grapes she held in her hand." "But this is the time of day when the sun touches the leaves with golden fingers and the grapes just inhale that warmth. They almost grow before your eyes."

Martha bent close to watch. Mary held up the cluster but didn't detach it from the vine.

"It's going to be another wonderful day," Mary declared, her face alight with the morning sunshine.

"Oh, how do you know that?" Martha objected. "Didn't you hear what happened in Jerusalem yesterday? An angry mob stampeded right up to the palace gates. Twenty people were killed by the soldiers. Everyone is going crazy. How can you say it's going to be another wonderful day?"

Mary looked at Martha, then across the gentle hills toward Jerusalem. "But Jesus is here," she said. "The Messiah."

"I know," Martha said. "I believe in Him, too. But . . ."

"He has a plan. Everything is going to turn out right. I just cling to that. He didn't say we wouldn't see trouble and difficulties. He even said that He would experience many of them. I don't understand it all," Mary added, "but I know He tells the truth."

"You're right, of course." Martha gave her a reluctant smile. "And I believe that, too. But I don't have the joy you have. What makes you so happy? You glow like the sunshine."

"I do?" Mary said, suddenly feeling shy. "I didn't realize that."

"Everyone sees it. And they say, 'What's going on with her?'"

Mary stared at the grapes covering the leafy vines. She ran her fingers over the plump, round balls of purple.

"Last week Deborah said that she and Hannah saw you at the well. They were rude, weren't they?"

Mary nodded. Her brows knit together and her eyes filled with tears. "I guess they just can't forget."

"Well, I've forgotten," she said emphatically, "and so has Jesus. And Lazarus. You are special, Mary. So special! And I'm glad you're my sister."

Mary looked up with a smile.

"But how do you manage to see the good in everything?" Martha asked. "You smile from deep inside.

Mary studied the grapes in her hand. Martha scanned the short, full vines that marched in neat rows over the hill. Clusters of fat, round grapes hung like jewels. They looked ready to burst, and she could almost taste their sweet juice trickling down her throat.

"What's happened to me is similar to what's happening to these grapes," Mary said after a long silence. She bent her head to inhale their sweet perfume. "Just as these beautiful grapes are growing and ripening, day after day joy is growing inside me. Sometimes I feel I'm about to burst, too." She pulled two grapes from the cluster, offered one to Martha, and they popped the sweet fruit into their mouths.

Mary felt the skin crunch between her teeth, then a burst of sweetness filled her mouth. She signed. "Wonderful!"

"Yes," Martha agreed.

"These juicy grapes exist because of the grapevine," Mary said, remembering one of the illustrations Jesus had given. "They hang from branches that are connected to the vine. Branches take strength and nourishment from the vine and—"

"And grapes just pop out," Martha laughed, making her hands into fists and flinging them open so that each finger shot out in a different direction.

Mary laughed too. "You are a genius," she said to her sister. She gently let go of the cluster and they headed back to the house.

"I'm just a grafted branch that needs more time to nurture my connection to the vine," Martha said.

"And I'll help you with the laundry so you'll have that time."

Martha watched Mary walk ahead of her on the path. She smiled when Mary stopped to straighten a lily that had fallen against a rock. Mary packed some dirt around the base of the plant with a satisfied smiled. Then Martha remembered the words of Jesus, "Unless you become as innocent, trusting, and harmless as this little child, you cannot even be admitted into God's kingdom. This innocence comes to adults only by choice." She shook her head. Mary, the guilty one had become like an innocent child. She took pleasure in each small wonder around her. That's why she went to the vineyard every morning. She was watching the miracle, and it was speaking to her heart.

"And I've been too busy to join her," Martha whispered.

A Mended Heart Produces Grapes

Jerusalem.

Not too long ago.

The sun had just peeked above the horizon and dew still sparkled on every flower and tree the morning I walked down a dusty road beyond our hotel overlooking the city of Jerusalem. My footsteps took me to a rock wall that surrounded a small vineyard. Entering through a gate in the wall, I was thrilled to stand beside a parade of vines in straight rows. A tower built of rocks stood in the center of the field, similar to the lookout towers that were built in fields when Jesus walked this earth.

I walked down a row, searching for clusters of grapes among the leaves. There they hung, tiny seed-like grapes clinging to the branches. I imagined Jesus standing there telling the crowd that followed Him, "I am the vine and you are the branches. I have arranged the branches over strong supports and trimmed them. Now I am looking for the fruit, the grapes." This experience fastened a great truth in my mind and heart: If I want the fruit of joy and peace in my life, I must connect, connect, *connect* with the Vine.

As a young child, I wanted to please my grandmother. I felt especially close to her and enjoyed going into her room and looking at all the beautiful things she had placed on her shelves. Each of them had been made by a grandchild or one of her children. I wanted to make something to add to her collection, something that would make her smile.

I remembered that Miss Smith had promised to help us create piggy banks on a certain Monday morning. I was excited, yet felt afraid that I would make a mess of the project.

"Grandma, I'll never be able to make a piggy bank from some old blob of clay," I cried. "Miss Smith is bringing clay to school tomorrow. I'm not going."

Grandma looked at me with sparkling blue eyes. She reached out a thin veined hand and patted mine. "You can do it!" she said with a firmness that startled me. "I believe you will do your best, and I know I will like your bank."

The next day, Teacher dropped a giant brown bag onto her desk. "As your name is called, you may come and get your lump of clay," she said, reaching into the bag and twisting off portions of clay for each of us.

Big Frank swaggered to the front. He grabbed a hunk of clay and carried it to his desk, letting brown liquid run down his elbows and drop onto the floor. He banged the clay onto his desk and attacked it with two knotted fists.

Susan inched to the front of the room. She extended both hands and grimaced when the wet clay touched her white skin. She held her hands as far from her pink ruffled dress as possible, and placed her lump on a sheet of white paper she'd placed on her desk. She stared at the oozing brown gunk that stayed on her hands, and wiggled her nose in disgust.

Harold covered the distance to the teacher's desk in two long strides. He grabbed his piece and began pushing it into shape even before he reached his desk. He poked it until his fingers disappeared into the soft mass, and rolled it into spaghetti. He formed a giraffe with an astounding long neck then flattened his masterpiece with one slap of a brown hand.

I pried my eyes from his rapidly changing clay mass when my name was called. I walked to the front determined to hide my fears and took the lump assigned to me, swallowing one that lodged in my throat. *I'll never make a pig that is useful much less something good to look at,* I thought. I wished I could run from the room. Instead I squinted, visualizing the form of a fat, jolly-faced pig with a curled tail. I pounded the clay, squeezed it, and rolled it until it felt flexible, then tried to shape that mental picture into reality. But, the clay refused to shape itself into a pig. Instead, it looked like a basketball with lips. I rolled it a bit to thin it down. Then it looked like a legless lizard with a walnut trapped inside. The minutes ticked away, and my clay blob came no closer to becoming a pig.

"Students, you have 10 minutes to finish up," Miss Smith stated as if she reluctantly held time open for a few of us who seemed less capable.

Desperately, I pinched off one end of my snake and smoothed it out until it resembled an elongated rhinoceros. The only remaining hollow place inside collapsed when I attempted to cut a slot. I ignored a sudden impulse to smash the horrid object into a pancake. What would I say to Grandma? She had the unshakable belief that a lot of prayer and determination could conquer anything. I felt sure that at that very moment she was home praying for my pig.

I daubed blue paint into the shape of a non-excitant flower to decorate each squat leg and outlined the pretend money slot with white lines. Time was up.

I glanced up nervously and saw that the other students sat admiring an assortment of piglike clay blobs. Big Frank sneered at Susan's pink piggy bank, and planted a blob of brown clay on a yellow curl that hung across her forehead.

"You've done very well," the teacher said, stopping her purposeful glance just short of my desk. I know your families will appreciate your hard work."

We carved our initials into the soft surface of the pigs' undersides, "So no one will get mixed up and take the wrong bank home," Teacher said. I felt sure no one would accidentally take my pig.

Far too soon the pigs had been baked and cooled. They stood staring at us and blaming us for their outcome. I quickly wrapped my rhinoceros in white tissue and tucked it into my lunch sack.

"It's wonderful!" Grandma exclaimed, holding the brown bank in her hands. "I'll just put it right here on my dresser."

"Oh, no, Grandma," I cried. "Put it into the drawer." I knew I couldn't face that misshaped pig every time I came into her small room.

"No, child," she said. "This is a 'You-can-do-it' pig. You did your best. The next time you will try harder and do better." She placed the bank on a frilly white doily.

Years later, I entered my grandmother's room shortly after her death at 96. I closed the door and sat alone in her sturdy rocking chair. There on her end table sat the clay pig. I knew she had placed it there during her last illness. It said that she knew I would miss her, miss the way she always counted on me to do my best, urging me to try harder.

"There's one thing you didn't tell me," Grandma, I sighed. "The truth is that everything I try to do will turn out just as my efforts to make a piggy bank—unless I allow our heavenly Potter to lay His hands over mine and to be the One who takes control and shapes my life.

My teacher missed a great opportunity to teach me this lesson. When she saw my struggle she could have come and placed her hands over mine, instead of leaving me to struggle alone. She could have helped me. Together we could have made a pig. Perhaps she didn't know the secret of the Potter either. Maybe she didn't sense my need or have the time or desire to lead me in this way. But God does. He helped me learn the wonderful truth that a changed heart is a gift, a result of His power. "But you are our Father, Lord. You are the potter and we are the clay. We are the work of your hands" (Isaiah 64:8).

The Potter knows the person you long to be. He promises to take you in His nail-scarred hands and reshape you. He knows that you will never be able to change your own life nor produce good works, like delicious grapes, on your own. He is full of joy that He can.

The answer to your problem is to allow Him to graft you to Himself, the vine, so its strength and life will surge through you and produce the good fruit of grapes. His solution is for you to stop trying and simply give Him permission to give you, as a gift, the miracle.

A Dead Reef Gets New Life

The red sun burst above the horizon, red as a pearl from a volcano. I dragged my dive bag from beneath the bench that hugged the length of our boat. I hung my dive suit over the side of the boat to soak it in the warm sea before wiggling into the wet, stretchy fabric.

My dive buddies unzipped their bags and began to sort through the pile of gear. No one spoke as we strapped on computers, knives, weight belts, and masks. We thrust our feet into boots and fins and our hands into gloves. We pulled out cameras and collecting bags, and double checked our vests that sat attached to full tanks of air.

We moved slowly in spite of our longing to leap off the end of the boat, rechecking every piece of equipment and wiping the sweat from our faces.

I grabbed one last drink of water, tossing the plastic bottle into my bag, and kicking it beneath the bench. Two awkward steps put me at the dive platform where I waited for my partner to join me.

"Don't forget," my friend Martha said. We had decided to take a record of the corals we saw. She clutched a dive slate in her left hand. A small pencil dangled from six inches of hollow tubing.

"Stash that pencil into its holder," I mumbled as I inched myself into position for the leap.

"Now!" the dive master shouted. I jumped into the water and disappeared beneath the surface.

"Your turn," the dive master called just as I surfaced and gave the OK signal. Martha leaped and splashed in beside me.

"Follow me," I said in dive signal language. Martha stared at my hands, palms flat, one thrust out before the other like two divers lined up. She swam in behind me, and we headed downward toward the reef at a gentle angle. We leveled off just above the corals that stretched out before us like a cluttered garden.

It looks so fantastic, I wanted to shout, but instead I pointed to a huge brain coral. It measured six feet across and sat like a giant pumpkin in a sandy field. I wanted to run my fingers along the grooves that snaked along its surface, but I knew it would injure the delicate coral polyps that produce the hard stony skeleton we call coral.

Martha marked a number 1 on the small slate. Beside the number she wrote, Boulder Brain Coral.

We slithered over the top of the reef and down through coral canyons. I felt amazed at the variety of coral. I discovered corals with short stubby fingers.

Finger coral, I signaled, holding up four fingers. Martha jotted that down.

Next we spotted beautiful pillar corals. Each thin pillar pointed upward as if to reach for the rays of sunlight that filtered down into the water.

Some coral looked like a thick skin creeping up and over rocks or other corals. Others looked like stars.

Martha jotted down the names as fast as we discovered them. Lettuce coral, she wrote when we rose along a wall at 25 feet and discovered a coral growing against the wall in irregular flat plates like different size dishes flung carelessly into a cupboard.

Next we swam across a barren lagoon toward the main reef. I practiced my kick technique, trying to slither along like a streamlined barracuda. Suddenly Martha jabbed me with her gloved hand and pointed at a gray mound far ahead of us.

We kicked our fins and moved toward the mound, discovering that it was actually a great pile of dead corals that lay strewn over the sand, gray and broken. Only a few small fish darted about. I touched the coral and a cloud of gray rose in the water.

"What happened?" I wanted to scream at Martha, but no sounds came. I grabbed her slate.

"Something destroyed this reef," I wrote, thinking that more than a blast of dynamite caused the wreckage.

"Hurricane," Martha scribbled. "Big hurricane."

We poked around in the coral rubble finding a few interesting shells, then turned and headed back to the boat.

"Something sure destroyed that patch reef," I gasped, flinging myself over the side of the boat. "There isn't a living coral around and hardly any fish."

Later as I sat in my hotel room, I read about what scientists call the "coral doctor." His purpose is to remove living coral from a living reef and place it into a container of seawater. This coral will become a transplant for a dead reef.

Next the coral doctor dives with a dive buddy into a dead reef, damaged by pollution, boat anchors, or storms. They search for a solid place for the transplant. The coral doctor prepares a smooth place on the reef while his buddy returns to the boat and reaches for a great glob of glue that resembles dough. He takes the glue and the live coral to the coral doctor.

After applying the glue, the coral doctor wiggles the living coral into place. Then the living coral grows and reproduces, scattering life throughout the dead reef. The fish return, as do all the other creatures that make a reef a place of great beauty.

You Can Receive a New Heart

What you and I really need is a transplant, a new heart. Jeremiah 24:7 says, "'I will give them . . . a heart that will know I am the Lord. They will be my people, and I will be their God, for they will love me with all their hearts.'"

This new heart can do three things that your old heart can't do, and it does them naturally. It comes filled with a strong love for Jesus. It likes spiritual things and is drawn to what is pure and holy. And the new heart's strongest desire is to serve others. This is true because of a new set of principles that God implants within you when you turn your life over to Him.

How Jesus Lives Within the New Heart

One morning just when the sun peeked over the horizon painting the sky red and gold, I leaped off the side of the dive boat and settled to the bottom of the sea 45 feet below. White sand stretched out beyond me like an underwater desert. I flipped my fins and glided across the lagoon toward the reef.

My friends and I had just arrived at Majuro, a tiny island that from the air looked like a donut with a bite taken out of it. We'd laid concrete block all morning, helping a group of young people construct a cafeteria and gymnasium, then in the afternoon we donned our SCUBA gear and jumped into the sea.

Groupers with fat lips floated past, and angel fish darted by. Suddenly I spotted a weird shell on the sea floor. I moved down to take a closer look. *Wow. A giant clam,* I thought. *It's big. It must easily weigh 400 pounds.*

Suddenly I remembered reading that a giant clam could snap shut on the foot of unwary divers, holding them to the sea floor until they drowned. Later I read that scientists decided even a giant clam couldn't do that because its shell couldn't close that tight. I decided to do a little experiment for myself. Holding my dive knife in one hand just in case I needed to cut myself free, I stuck my hand into the clam. It snapped quickly shut. I felt the soft flesh of the clam press against my hand, but my hand easily slipped free. The scientists were right.

Next I decided to look the giant clam over to discover how such a great creature could secure enough food to grow so large. While I stared at it, a tiny crab scurried up the outside of the shell and stood on the edge of its opening. *This crab is about to become supper,* I thought. But instead of swallowing the crab, the clam jerked its shells enough to give a message to the crab. "Get yourself off my shell," it seemed to say. The crab lost no time scurrying away. *I guess it doesn't eat small critters,* I thought.

I swam off to check out another creature when I saw a small

giant clam wedged between two corals. I tried breaking the clam loose, but it had glued itself to the corals. This clam wasn't going shopping for supper. I noticed that it had no claws, no tentacles, not even a small harpoon with which to reach out and grab food swishing past on the currents. *How does this giant thing eat?* I wondered.

As I stared at the shell, I saw it open up. I saw thick flesh along its edges. It looked like a person's lips, all soft and puckered up. I knew that this flesh is called a mantle because I'd seen it in other bivalve shells.

By this time my air gauge signaled me to get back to the surface. When I reached the boat, I wiggled out of my gear, dried off, and opened my identification book. "Clams," the book said, "open up to the sunshine inviting green algae to enter its tissue and set up farming. The algae can gather up the tiny wispy rays of sun that seep down into the reef and create food for the giant clam."

Colossians 1:27 says, "God wants to use you to attract others to Him with the glorious riches of what has been revealed and which is seen by Christ living in you, who is our only living hope of glory."

The Heart Mender wants you to live a life that attracts others to Him. The way He does this is a mystery. But the mystery has been revealed, opened to your understanding. Your hope of a glorious future—the possibility of a healed heart—is reality because of the indwelling Jesus in your life. He actually becomes the Heavenly Algae, living within your heart. This is a stunning idea. As the giant clam opens itself to the green algae, bringing life-giving food to the clam, open your heart to receive Jesus so that He can create a new heart in you, producing life.

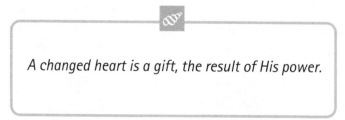

A changed heart is a gift, the result of His power.

A Lesson in Mending

For months I searched for the Atlantic triton trumpet shell. I snorkeled along the thin line of reef that fringed Miller's Beach in the Bahamas. I plodded across sand bars far from shore, looked under rocks strewn over the sea floor, and poked between clustered corals in the reef.

"The triton trumpet is one of your best creations," I whispered to God. "I just have to find one."

Then one morning four friends and I stuffed ourselves into a jeep and jogged over a rutted road to a distant Bahamas beach. We waded in waist deep water, searching the coral garden for treasure. I had almost forgotten about the triton trumpet.

Suddenly I saw the tip of a shell. It looked pink as a rose. "A triton trumpet," I shouted to Anita who searched nearby.

"Pull it out," she screamed, dancing about in the water.

Holding my breath, I took hold of that pink tip and drew it slowly out of the crevice. *Is it just a piece of broken shell, or a perfect triton trumpet?* I thought. Finally I couldn't wait another moment to know the truth. I yanked, and the whole shell came out.

"She's got one," Anita yelled. "A whole triton trumpet! Our friends splashed over to us. They gathered around to see my prize.

"What a beautiful shell," they chorused.

"Now to find the Pacific triton trumpet," I said, "It's even lovelier than this one."

A year later my friends and I flew to Majuro Island in the South Pacific. We joined a crew of young people who wanted to build a new school for the children who lived on this beautiful island. We worked in the mornings, and in the afternoons we snorkeled and dove into the lagoon, searching for treasure.

"God, I know the Pacific triton trumpet that lives here is the most beautiful triton of all. I want to show people what a fantastic Creator you are. Please help me find one," I prayed.

I searched and I prayed, waiting for the moment my eyes would discover the Pacific triton trumpet in its hiding place. I could almost feel the smooth, shinny surface and see the lines and bars that made up its fancy patterns. But I did not find the trumpet, and I wondered why God did not answer my prayer.

From Trash to Treasure

At about the same time, far across the sea, a small boy whose name I may never know prayed that God would help him find a beautiful treasured triton.

One morning just as the sun squeezed itself over the horizon splashing streaks of red and blue on the canvass of the sky, the boy and his father pushed a little wooden boat across the wet sand toward the splashing waves. They shoved the boat hard and watched it lift up onto the mounds of water, then they jumped in and rowed with all their might until they cleared the line of breakers.

Once out onto the smooth water of the lagoon they put bait on several lines and threw them out into the sea. The father watched the lines. When one became taught, he jerked the line and pulled in a fish.

The boy prepared to dive. He did not own fins, a mask, or an air tank. Instead, he wore a ragged pair of trunks, goggles, and a smile.

"I'm going to find a triton trumpet, Father," he called as he leaped from the boat and sank down through the azure water. He darted about the scattered corals like a reef fish, looking into every crevice, then along the reef edges and across the white sand patches. The Caribbean sun awakened the day as the boy dove and returned to the surface over and over again.

"I just have to find one," he said to his father as he rested, hanging his arms over the side of the boat. The hours passed. The boy flushed a flounder from its hiding place in the sand and followed a fat grouper around a huge brain coral, but he didn't see the treasured triton.

Then, just as the sun touched the western horizon the boy spotted two mounds on the white sand of the ocean floor. He dove, kicking hard. He grabbed the mounds. Triton trumpets, his mind screamed. *Two trumpets.*

He tucked one shell under each arm and headed for the boat floating just above him.

"Dad!" he screamed as he burst through the surface. "Two triton trumpets. I found them just sitting on the sand."

His father reached down, took the shells from his son's hands, and pulled the boy into the boat.

The man stared at the shells. "They're really big ones," he said at last.

"The biggest ones I've ever seen!" the boy said happily. "May I keep them?"

"We've got room for them," His father said, "but they don't look like much. See how they're covered with gray silt that has hardened over the months. Someone fishing out here probably pried out the snail and tossed the shells overboard.

The boy frowned. He took the triton from his father's hands.

"Dad, I searched a long time for these shells. I know they look awful, but I want to take them home. There must be some way to make them pretty again."

The father nodded and they drew in the fish lines and paddled home with a boat full of fish and the two tritons.

The boy cleaned the shells, but he couldn't remove the ugly silt layer from their surface. Even so, he placed the dull shells on a shelf in his room, turning them so he could see the bit of color that peeked from the inside.

"I want to clean these up," he told his mother. "I know there must be a way. Then they will be beautiful."

"Perhaps God will show you a way," Mother said. "Go wash up, we are having a very important visitor tonight."

All through supper the boy thought about what gift he could give their guest, a man by the name of Elder Bob Folkenberg. "I don't have anything valuable," he sighed to himself.

Then some words grabbed the boy's attention. ". . . and my wife just loves shells," Elder Folkenberg was saying.

The boy jumped up and ran to his room.

He returned carrying the two sea shells.

"I want you to take these shells home to your wife," he told their visitor.

Elder Folkenberg looked at the tritons. "They're very big," he said, complimenting their size and ignoring the ugliness of the outer covering. "Thank you very much."

Arriving home, he unpacked the shells and handed them to his wife, Anita. "Triton trumpets," she said in surprise. "But they are hopelessly crusted."

Anita called me, and I headed for her house to see the gift. *At last God has answered my prayer for a Pacific triton trumpet,* I thought.

"These look hopeless," Anita said, holding up the two huge shells as I came in the door. "But there must be some way to clean them."

"They surely *are* ugly," I agreed. Disappointment grabbed my throat.

"It doesn't look like it has a bit of color left," Anita said with a sigh, "but, maybe you can find a way to clean it up." So saying, she thrust one of the tritons into my hands.

At home I soaked the triton in bleach overnight. The next morning I rinsed it off and started to scrape it with sharp dental tools. Scrape, scrape, scratch, scrape. The sounds of scraping could be heard all over the house. Day after day I soaked and scraped. My fingers hurt. I got behind in my work. But I didn't care. I had to know if that shell could be cleaned and if some of the beautiful pattern God created in it still existed beneath the crust. I worked on the shell every day for the next three weeks.

Finally I'd done all I could. I dipped the shell one last time and dried it off. I mixed together one ounce of lighter fluid and three ounces of baby oil, then poured some of the solution into my hands. I picked up the shell, and then, as carefully as a mother rubs a baby's body, I rubbed the solution over every inch of the triton.

I stared at the miracle before me. The shell that had been thrown away—trashed, as useless—had been found and changed into a thing of beauty.

"And this can be your miracle, too," God whispered into my heart.

It can also be yours.

Forgiven One, rest in the hands of the Great Shell Collector. Rest and look. While you look, He will cleanse you and change you into a thing of beauty. This is His gift.

Now that you have the new heart that loves God, you will respond to that love in a new and wonderful way.

I stared at the miracle before me. The shell had been found, and changed into a thing of beauty.

CHAPTER NINE

The Response of a Mended Heart

The wounded heart heals slowly.
Nights of agony fade into mornings of peace.

MARY, MESSENGER FOR GOD

A faint light shone above the horizon and a rooster crowed as Mary wrapped herself in a shawl and tiptoed from the house. Outside, she hurried down the stony path, through town, past the well, and toward the garden. She stumbled, and brushed away tears with the back of her hand. But the tears flowed down her cheeks as she thought of the past few days. Jesus—her heart's hope and the joy of her life—had been crucified. The One who healed the sick and awakened the dead now slept in a tomb.

She missed His laughter. That He was dead—*dead!*—seemed impossible.

Rays of sunlight crept across the pathway, but she didn't see them. The world seemed dark. She could not even imagine light.

She'd believed He was the Son of God. Hadn't He wept at her brother's tomb then called him to life with a command! Her brother had literally walked from the grave into life. How could it be that Jesus had power over death, yet did nothing to save His own life? She didn't understand it. She remembered the times He'd tried to talk to them about . . . about death, His death . . . crucifixion, but it was unthinkable. They'd all but put their hands over their ears, but now she wondered and remembered. For a moment Mary wondered if all this fit together as part of a plan.

I must hurry, she thought, pushing these thoughts aside. *Mary and Salome are waiting. They have spices and perfumes for Jesus' body. I have nothing for Him.* She sighed, then a little feeling of joy swept through her. I'm glad I poured the spikenard over His feet at Simon's feast. I know that He knew how much I wanted to honor Him.

She ran past the well and arrived at the garden. Salome and Mary were probably already there. One glance told her that the stone had been rolled from the opening. She stopped to touch the petal of a white lily then quickened her pace. Her heart pounded. *Strange,* she thought, *I'm glad to be going to see Jesus even though He's dead.* Then the memory of His bruised body hanging limp from the terrible spikes forced the tears to flow again. She stumbled on.

"Salome, I'm here," she called stepping up to the tomb. Where were they? Maybe they hadn't arrived, after all. She stooped and looked inside the grave carved into the stone hillside. "What?" Her hand flew to her mouth. The tomb was empty. The linen cloth that John had wrapped about Jesus' face lay neatly folded at the head of the rock shelf. She touched it reverently. This had touched His precious face. Then she saw the body cloths lying at the far end of the shelf. Someone had taken the time and care to carefully fold them too.

She lingered for a heartbeat before shock propelled her out of the grave. "He's gone!" she shouted. "Someone has stolen His body."

Mary ran toward town.

"I must tell the disciples."

She passed the well.

"He's gone. His body is gone!"

Two women, drawing water, called out to her, but she didn't hear them over the pounding of her heart. The tomb was empty and someone had taken Him away. She repeated the thought over and over. Her grief, already great, deepened. She hurried into town and when she reached the upper room where the disciples hid, she hammered on the door. "Let me in." she cried. "It's Mary."

The door opened a narrow crack and John's face appeared. Mary pushed on the door and burst into the room. "They stole His body. He is gone," she screamed, throwing herself into John's arms. "I saw the empty tomb."

The disciples all spoke at once. They shook their heads. One looked out a window. Others laughed at the ridiculousness of it. "She's overwrought," one said.

"Of course," said another. "Jesus is there. We saw the stone rolled over the opening. No one could open that tomb with a legion of soldiers standing guard."

"I didn't see a single soldier," Mary wept. "And I couldn't find Salome or Mary."

The room fell quiet. John paced the wooden floor. Suddenly he stopped.

"Do you remember that Jesus said He would rise again?" John asked, looking from one to the other. "Could it be that—?"

Suddenly John pushed past Mary. "I'm going to the tomb," he called over his shoulder.

Peter spun after him. "I'm coming, too."

Mary watched them run down the street. She turned and looked about the room. She saw confusion, hope, fear, and doubt in the disciples' eyes. She hesitated then ran down the stairs and into the street. She passed shops just opened for the morning trade. Storekeepers called a greeting, others called a question, but she didn't give them a word or glance. Women still clustered about the well, but she ignored them.

"Mary," Hannah cried, "where are you going?"

But Mary didn't see Hannah nor hear her greeting. She thought only of the empty tomb. What did it mean? Surely someone had stolen the body because they thought it unworthy to be buried in the tomb of Joseph, wealthy man that he was.

Her face red from exertion, her breath coming in ragged gasps, she reached the yawning doorway where the Teacher had been placed just two days before. "It's just as you told us," Peter told her, his face pale with fear. He pointed to the empty stone shelf.

John placed his hand on her shoulder. "Don't worry, Mary. We'll find where they've put His body or if—"

"Let's get back to the others," Peter told him. "We must decide what to do."

Mary watched the men walk back up the path. Their shoulders slumped, and they did not speak. She started to follow, then stopped. She couldn't pull herself from the tomb. *This is the last place I saw Him,* she thought. *Perhaps one of the gardeners will know what happened to His body.* She turned back to the rock hewn doorway and stepped inside. Two men stood there, one at each end of the stone shelf.

"Woman, why do you weep?" one asked.

"Someone has taken away my Lord. I don't know where they have laid Him," she blurted, bursting into tears. Surely they knew that Jesus had been crucified and placed in this very tomb. She tried to focus on the two men. Their voices sounded kind. Finally she turned and walked back into the garden.

"Why are you weeping? Who are you looking for?" someone asked.

Mary wiped her eyes with the sleeve of her robe. She looked up and saw a man. *The gardener,* she thought. *Surely he will know where Jesus' body has been taken.*

"Sir," she said, "if you have taken Jesus away, please tell me where you laid Him. Lazarus' tomb is empty since Jesus raised him from the dead. I'll put Jesus there. He'll be safe."

"Mary."

Mary froze. She knew that voice. Brushing the tears from her eyes, she looked up into the smiling face of Jesus. She flung herself at His feet.

"Wait," Jesus said. "Don't be afraid. It's true. It's me, but I must go to my Father"—He paused—"and to your Father, too. Then I'll return. But go tell My disciples that I am alive. I have risen from the dead just as I said I would."

"Lord!" Mary cried, covering her face with her hands. When she looked up moments later, He was gone. She stared at the path where He had stood.

"Go and tell," He had said. "Go!"

She leaped to her feet and ran through the garden, her hair flying and her sandals kicking up a cloud of dirt. Up the pathway she ran, down the street. Passing the well, she spotted

Hannah tugging to lift a dripping water pot.

"Hannah," she cried. "He's alive! Jesus has risen from the dead. I saw Him."

She didn't stop to hear the woman's reply. She kept running. She passed a bakery where a man peered through a small window. "He's alive," she called. In the sandal shop, hammers stopped tapping when she cried out, "He's alive." The butcher stood in the doorway of his shop wiping his hands on an ample apron. "Mary, hello," he called to her.

"Jesus has risen from the dead," she cried again and again. "I saw Him. I spoke to Him."

Men and women stepped aside to let her pass. "Jesus is alive," she shouted. "The tomb is empty." They could only stare after her retreating form.

Her sorrow flew away on the morning breeze. His voice, like a tender hand, had passed over her heart. The grief-gouged chasm in her heart now overflowed with joy. Yes, Jesus had suffered terribly, but now He lived. He was the Son of God. She would tell everyone! She ran up the steps to the upper room and banged on the door.

Our Response to His Mending

Often the wounded heart heals slowly. Nights of agony fade into mornings of peace, as grief releases its hold upon the heart. Then a day comes when you know you have changed. You have become a different person—confident, hopeful, and at peace. This is the time when the Heart Mender gently nudges you, as He did Mary, on an errand. He gives you a mission. He says, "Go! Go tell others what I have done for you."

Moving you from grief to gratitude is a wonderful process, one at which the Heart Mender excels. The first nine verses of Isaiah 6 will help you gain insight into His methods. Here Isaiah reveals how Jesus healed his soul, then said, "Go." Isaiah tells his story to enable you to understand your own experience. The recorded portion of Isaiah's journey toward God begins when he sees God in a vision, looking into the very throne room of God. The drama begins in Isaiah 6:1.

"There I saw the Lord sitting on a throne, high and lifted up, and His presence filled the place with glory."

Isaiah wastes no time telling you what happened to him. He saw God. In verses 2 and 3 he describes the wonder of the heavenly throne room filled with glorious light. He recounts his awe as angels fold their wings and shout, "Glory, glory, glory."

God brought Isaiah into the throne room to give him a clear picture of His purity, power, and love. Then He instructed Isaiah to record it so that you and I, who may not receive a personal vision, could also see God.

What happened to Isaiah after he came face to face with God astonished me. I think you will be surprised too. Imagine, for a moment, that your eyes have just feasted on the face of God. Wouldn't you be excited, astonished, and awed? Wouldn't you join the angels bursting into song? An experience like that would set you dancing. But look what it did to Isaiah. After he saw God he cried out, " 'I'm gone. There's no hope for me! I am a man of unclean lips. I have sinned. My own nature can't be trusted and I live among a sinful people. I am doomed, for my eyes have seen the King, the Lord Almighty, the God of Israel.' "

One minute Isaiah gazes at glory, the next he sees only darkness. First he looks into the face of God, then he discovers he is a sinner. The songs of angel voices are followed by moans from his own throat. What he saw and heard in that throne room was such a contrast with what he saw in himself that it threw him on his face before God and wrenched the statement, "I am doomed," from his lips. But the story doesn't end with Isaiah face down on the floor.

Immediately, Isaiah uses the word *then*. This word tells you that something else is about to happen. Read it with me.

"*Then* I saw one of the angels take a burning coal from the altar of incense in the heavenly Sanctuary, fly down to where I was, and touch my lips with this live coal. As he did so he said, 'This coal represents God's grace. Atonement has been made for your sins and your guilt has been removed' " (Isaiah 6:6, 7).

Did you catch the fantastic good news in these verses? Watch the angel fly from God's throne room to Isaiah's side. Gasp as the angel holds a white hot coal against his lips. Then shout for joy when you hear the message, " 'This coal represents God's grace. Atonement has been made for your sins and your guilt has been removed.' "

Isaiah arose and accepted the free gift of grace. He believed that his guilt was gone.

You can accept the experience of Isaiah as your own, delivered to you, personally, from God. You can see God in nature, within the Word, and as you talk with Him. Beholding Him you will be amazed at His power and awed by His radiance. Then you will be faced by your own sinfulness, your rebellion and fear. What you won't see are fingers pointing at you. What you won't hear are words of condemnation. The awesomeness of unconditional love and grace will throw you on your face before Him. Then at His command, angels who stand in His presence will be sent with the gift of grace, declaring that your sins are forgiven. You will *know* your guilt is gone.

If you feel like putting this book down right now and jumping up and down, I'll understand. Go ahead and shout, "Glory, glory, glory to God."

But, wonder of wonders, the story does not end here. You see, Isaiah saw something else. Read the first part of verse 8.

"Then I heard the voice of the Lord, saying, 'Whom shall I send to my people? Who will go for me and be my messenger?' "

At this moment, the scene changes. Isaiah now turns from his own experience and discovers the needs of others. God is calling for help. He needs a messenger. He does not demand. He asks, "Who will go?"

Isaiah does not hesitate. "Here am I, Lord," he says. "Send me." He's ready, willing, and eager even though he doesn't have a clue about what He just agreed to do. He knows that God needs help. He knows that God is searching for a messenger.

Isaiah says, "Send me." Just like that. I found this amazing, then I read again the phrase that preceded Isaiah's "send me" statement. Take a look at it because here he describes the reason for his willingness. He says, "With my heart overflowing with gratitude for what the Lord had done for me, I said, 'Here am I, Lord. Send me.' "

Not all Bible versions portray this so clearly, but gratitude always bursts from a heart that experiences grace. It becomes the driving force behind a life of service. Isaiah is ready. He wants to go. He asks to go. He seeks to discover what he can do for God.

As soon as Isaiah admits his willingness to go, God says, " 'Then go and give my people this message . . .' " In the next 60 chapters Isaiah records these messages from God. They are pregnant with love, desire, forgiveness, hope, and love.

Take another look at this fantastic process:

> He saw God.
>
> He saw his sinfulness.
>
> He saw God's grace.
>
> He saw a need.
>
> He saw his mission.

Now enter into the process yourself. Begin where Isaiah did. You must "see" God.

Three things I can do to help me "see" God are:

_____

_____

_____

_____

I have discovered that Jesus is:

_____

_____

_____

_____

Now, look at yourself in contrast to what you see in Jesus. Make it an honest glance. Ask God to show you your true condition.

When I consider the pure life of Jesus, I see these things in myself and I feel:

_____

_____

_____

_____

Now turn your eyes away from your situation, your sin, and your past. Look into the face of unconditional love and forgiveness. Accept the coal that represents grace. Say aloud, "I accept the unconditional love of Jesus and His grace." This means

_____

_____

_____

_____

Now realize that, perhaps slowly, a new adventure will begin. The God who rescued you also has a plan for your life. His plan will fit perfectly. He will disclose it to you in His own time and way, but you can begin to pray, "Show me a need that I can respond to. Help me discover your gifts."

My Response to His Love

When I surrendered my future to Jesus all over again I took one more time to honestly admit my losses. Then I turned to look at what I had left. I had the love of my children, many friends, myself, health, my education, and a renewed zest for life. Still I had no idea what to do with the rest of my life.

Now *you*. Stop a moment. I have just returned to this portion of my story to tell you a little more of the truth about where God found me when He said, "Go!" The reason I am doing this is that I want you to know that it is of absolutely no consequence what your situation is right now. Your life is not about what you have lost, or even what you have left. When you choose Him, you have aligned yourself up with the Almighty God who has everything and knows everything. That's the key.

I was not in a good situation when God said to me, "Go." I was still reeling from the loss of my marriage, my role as a pastor's wife, loss of friends, and of financial security. I lived in a home that was no longer mine and had only a few weeks to find other housing. Yet I had no money to enable me to move. Because I had made the ministry my fulltime work, I had no job or career to turn to.

I lay on a couch with my foot in a cast, still groggy from surgery. I couldn't even walk to the bathroom—I had to crawl. My phone had been turned off and the electric company threatened to cut the service.

But just as He had Isaiah, God had been preparing me without my realizing it, by putting me through the process. I had reaffirmed my choice to walk with God, spent weeks reading the Gospels, spent time in nature gazing at His beautiful creation, and poured my heart out to Him. I had surrendered myself to His keeping, and I had seen His grace. I received His peace, believing with my whole being that He had a plan, though I had no clue what it could be.

God sent people to help me in a hundred ways. They called to encourage me, to make suggestions, and to remind me that God was in control. One church member handed me enough money to make the needed move. Another helped me pack. My sons loaded my things into a truck, and my best friend, Martha, offered her basement apartment to me until I could decide where I wanted to live permanently.

Then one morning, a principal of a large Christian school called. "The speaker for our spring week of prayer had to cancel. I've heard that you SCUBA dive and tell some pretty exciting stories that could benefit our students. Could you come to our school next week?"

I almost fainted when I heard myself say, "Yes. I will come."

That week exploded with activity. "What shall I do?" I asked God. "What do I have to say? I am not exactly in the best condition myself."

He answered with a question: "What do you have in your hands?"

"I have shells that teach beautiful lessons, a love for kids, lots of adventures, and a great desire to share," I responded. So the program Kids Can Know God was born. I built my presentations upon the lessons I learned from the Bible and my diving experiences in the bottom of the sea. I dragged myself to the computer and invented an activity book. My son David designed beautiful covers and posters for my program. I printed out the workbook pages and bound them with plastic spiral binders. Then I got the idea to share the many shells that I'd collected. I chose five that I could work into my talks, placing them—with sand—into pint plastic jars. I thought these "pocket beaches" would provide visual reminders of the lessons I wanted to teach. I was ready to "go."

God touched the hearts of those students. I was amazed by their joy and enthusiasm at learning about Jesus in this new way. They loved the "pocket beaches," and I thought, *Why not try this again?* Martha encouraged me to send out brochures to the area where she lived. I sent out six brochures describing my program. Within weeks I had six requests and six deposits. I used the deposits to purchase jars, sand, paper, shells, and printer ink. I set to work.

Many well meaning friends suggested that I get a job and live a normal life again. Their words made sense, but I had heard the call. I didn't know how things would work out, but I had some good years left and I wanted to give them to the Heart Mender. I would have to trust in His care for my future needs. Using his computer and artistic skills, David helped me develop attractive covers, advertisements, video inserts, and a hundred other things. But the most important gift he gave me was to encourage me to stay with my mission in spite of the risk it entailed. Now eight years and 300 seminars later I am still saying to God, "Send me!"

I found God to be an absolutely amazing partner, faithful in every way. He provided me with everything I needed to make preparing materials and traveling possible—a car, computers, printers, supplies, appointments, books, ideas, and courage. With every difficulty, He sent solutions. He bumped me into people who helped me print books, helped me travel, and purchase equipment. He didn't give me what I needed all at once, but just as I discovered a need He sent help. I experienced outright miracles over and over. I am so thrilled about how He has led in this adventure that I plan to write a book about it so others will have the courage to live their mission.

This fact blows me away. When I saw myself as middle-aged, abandoned, and unable to continue the life I had known, God saw something else. He saw me living an adventure beyond my wildest dreams. And He designed the new adventure to fit my personality, talents, and desires. I didn't have to force myself to respond to His call.

Where I needed to learn, He sent teachers.
When I lost courage, He sent hope.
Because I was alone, He drew near.

*I found God to be an
amazing partner, faithful in every way.*

Your Response to His Love

When you choose to come under the love and guidance of the Heart Mender, He sends a gift of immeasurable value to you. This gift is real, alive, and powerful. His name is Holy Spirit. His role in your life is multifaceted. Every day you will discover new and exciting things about Him. He's your comforter, teacher, guide, helper, and more. He brings two special gifts that will assist you in your new life.

The first gift is called fruit. God calls it fruit because it is the natural result of the presence of the Holy Spirit just as apples are the end result of the apple tree receiving rain, sun, and nutrients.

Galatians 5:22-24 tells us: "But the fruit which the Holy Spirit produces is . . . love, joy, peace, patience, kindness, generosity, faithfulness, humility, and self-control. There is no law against such things. Those who belong to Christ have crucified their sinful human nature and are no longer under its control."

This fruit is a gift—or result—of the indwelling Holy Spirit.

Love	Generosity
Joy	Faithfulness
Peace	Humility
Patience	Self-control
Kindness	

You don't deserve this fruit, and there is absolutely nothing you

can do to earn it. But with a grateful heart you can reach out and receive it as a free gift. And you can watch it ripen day by day under
the sunshine of His presence. This is a totally awesome experience.

The second great gift of the Holy Spirit is called "spiritual gifts."
You will find a discussion of them in 1 Corinthians 12.

The Holy Spirit brings gifts when He comes into your life. He
chooses the gifts with consideration to who you are—your back-
ground, your desires, abilities, and dreams. These, as stated in
1 Corinthians 12 include wisdom, knowledge, healing, faith, miracles, prophecy, languages, discernment, and teaching.

"Concerning spiritual gifts, I don't want you to be ignorant
about why they've been given to to us." "It's true that there are different gifts, but they all come from the same Holy Spirit. There are
different ministries, but we all serve the same Lord" (1 Corinthians
12:1, 4, 5).

Paul wants you to understand an important fact. The Holy Spirit
gives special abilities to each follower of Jesus. These are given so
that you will have a unique way of helping others and so that you
will be blessed as you use them. When I began to speak to children,
I learned to make the Gospel simple and captivating. Kids responded
to me in ways that brought further healing to my broken heart.
Their pictures, hugs, and delight poured over my wounded soul. I
gave, and I received much more in return. The amazing thing is that
each adult seminar I teach and every week of prayer I give, is new
and wonderful even after eight years.

Two years into my mission adventure I read an amazing book ti-
tled *The Path,* by Laurie Beth Jones. (Jones is the author of the best
selling book, *Jesus, CEO.*) In extremely practical terms it outlined
how to discover and practice a life of passion and mission. I learned
how to develop a mission statement and that I should establish my
work on a sensible platform of faith, prayer, and planning. This delightful and powerful book can help you discover and use your spiritual gifts.

God is more than willing to give these gifts to you through the
Holy Spirit. Just ask Him, then trust Him to know what gift is best.
Ask Him to teach you about yourself, your personality, your abili-

ties, and to help you discover the best way for you to serve Him.

Consider a mountain meadow. Silver-edged grass sways in the breeze, jays call from the treetops, water leaps over rocks, flowers sway in gold and blue clusters, and clouds tumble past on a blue canvass sky. A beaver glides across the pond and cuts a tree as easily as a child picks a wildflower, while butterflies soar on fragile wings.

The whole scene is made wonderful because of the variety and because each creature and plant is living out its mission. The beaver never says, "I am tired of building dams. I want to pollinate flowers." If it did this, the flowers would be trampled. Nor does a butterfly say, "I am not worth much, flitting all around the meadow. I want to build a dam."

"Nonsense!" you say. Yet how often we enter into work that we are ill suited, for or we expect that God will ask us to do something that we will not want to do. The Creator of the mountain meadow knows what He is doing. Trust Him.

The Heart Mender has plans for your life. He watched you come into this world. He followed your baby steps when you learned to walk. He laughed when you turned your face up to catch the rain, when you picked wild flowers by a brook and ran your toes through sand at the seashore.

He knows the dreams and hopes that formed within your heart. He weeps at your pain, understands your fears, and forgives your failures. He set a plan in motion to rescue you and give you new purpose. Age, looks, money, talents, past failures—none of these matter. What matters is that—today—you put yourself into the hands of the Heart Mender.

I want to suggest another book that has impacted my life in an extreme way. Reading it will add a richness and blessing to your life that you can't yet imagine. I invite you acquaint yourself with the Heart Mender by reading *The Desire of Ages* by Ellen G. White. This book is by far the best and most important book I have ever read. I read it cover to cover every year. Each time I read it I focus on a particular theme such as the character of Christ, His teaching methods, how He treated people, His promises, or His special requests. Ellen White, a woman with little education, wrote this book in her middle years after a lifetime of walking with Jesus, serving people, establishing schools and hospitals, traveling, and counseling. She saw God, and she wrote about what she saw.

Her book takes you on an intimate journey with the Savior. You'll see Him lying in a manger, walking on water and touching lepers. You'll hear Him teaching on a mountainside, commanding demons to leave their victims, and singing in a carpenter shop. Your heart will leap as He lays His hand on a child, brings a daughter to life, and gives up His life on a cross. Buy this book and read it for the rest of your life, side by side with the four Gospels. As you read it each year, like me you will come to know Him better, develop a gratitude for His plan of salvation, and join Him in the great adventure of helping others discover their God. From a heart full of gratitude you will say, "Send me."

Shark!

When I am tempted to be afraid, worried, or to lose courage, I close my eyes and visualize an amazing creature living so deep in the sea that your eyes will never see it, yet whose life paints a picture of the Heart Mender on the heart.

"Leap!" the dive master shouted as I stood wobbling on the platform at the end of the dive boat.

I stuck my right foot forward and plunged in. My dive buddy, Martha, followed. We gave each other the OK signal, sank to the bottom of the sea, and began to follow the shoreward edge of the reef.

Suddenly I spotted the shadowy form of a shark. It lingered nearby, watching us. I glanced at Martha. She reached out, grabbed my arm, and hung on. At that moment I realized I could do absolutely nothing for either of us. We were alone in the sea with a monster. I longed to dash into a steel shark cage and slam the door, but I merely hung there in the water, waiting to see its pectoral fins turn down and its back arch high, the signs of impending attack.

Long moments later, the shark swam away toward the open sea. Martha and I headed for the boat. We climbed in and sank onto a bench, not speaking. After drying off, I picked up my sea creature identification guide. Gray Reef Shark, the first picture shouted. I slammed the book shut.

The Tower of Safety

"Look at this," Martha said, shoving her book under my nose. A tiny creature with spindly legs looked up at me.

"That's just how I felt today," I said, "small, alone, and utterly helpless." Then I read something that erased my fear and sent me boldly back into the water.

Imagine, for a moment, that you're a spongecola shrimp, the tiny creature in my dive book. Your eyes pop open and you realize that you've just been born. You look at yourself and see that your body is nothing more than a speck of gelatin bobbing about in a great ocean. Legs, as thin as human hair, stick out from your sides.

You look around. You aren't floating on the surface where the sun paints the water gold. No sunbeams warm your back. You can't see the reef where rainbow-colored fish swish past and sea fans nod into the current. You see only blackness.

Suddenly a gulper fish—a snakelike creature with a head the size of a grapefruit—bursts out of the darkness. Its open mouth is ablaze with bioluminescent light. You're seized by terror and your heart cries out, *Is there no safe place?* You feel helpless. Fear drives you to dive down as the predator soars past and disappears into the darkness. Then the flash of light it leaves behind dims, and you are alone.

Fear drives you deeper and deeper into the blackness. At 10,000 feet you bump into a rock on the sea bottom. Then a voice speaks inside your brain. *Go find the tower,* it commands. You spin around in a full circle, searching. Suddenly you see something fastened to a rock with silver threads. It looks like a hollow tower made of spun glass threads woven together. It stands white against the blackness. *This is your safe place,* the voice whispers.

You tiny heart thumps as you swim to the tower and squeeze through an opening in the mesh walls just as another lighted predator flashes past.

A delicious sense of safety envelopes you. You swirl around in circles until you reach the top of the tower, then plunge down to the bottom. Suddenly you discover another spongecola shrimp hiding in the tower. Now, you're not alone.

Tiny particles of food filter through openings in your tower home, and you reach out and grab them, enjoying a plankton feast. You breathe in the molecules of oxygen that pepper the water. Suddenly you realize a great truth. Within the tower you have found everything you have ever needed. Your fear and loneliness float away on the sea current.

The Heart Mender

But you're *not* a spongecola shrimp. You're a woman cast, at birth, into a sin-darkened world. When you discover that Satan, the predator, cruises the reef of your life determined to destroy you, fear drives you to search for safety. You might attempt to build a safe place by seeking financial security, status, education, talent, career, success, and even the heart of a friend. But when these crumble, you cry out, "Is there no safe place?"

The resounding cry of the Bible is, yes! Proverbs 18:10 (NKJV) says that "The name of the Lord is a strong tower; the righteous run into it, and are safe."

The spongecola shrimp has its tower and you have Jesus. He is like a strong tower, one that cannot fall. How do I know this? Follow His story through the pages of the Bible and see for yourself.

Look at the infant, Jesus, destined to be our safe Tower, sleeping on a bed of straw. King Herod, filled with jealous rage, sees Him as easy prey. He sends soldiers to rampage through Bethlehem. Their horse's hooves kick up dust and their swords plunge through the hearts of infants. But God has already snatched His Son from death and hidden Him.

Listen to the lies Satan whispers to Jesus who is weak and hungry after 40 days without food. Satan tempts Him to give up the rescue plan for the human race, a plan that includes His own death on a Cross. But God strengthens Him and gives victory.

Observe the maddened crowd in Nazareth pushing Him toward a precipice. God hides Him from their eyes, and He passes through the crowd unharmed.

Follow the knot of priests, rulers, and lawyers who hound His every step. They seek to trap Him and find an excuse to end His holy life. God gives Him wisdom to triumph over His enemies.

Consider the sophistry of Satan, who enrages men to nail Jesus to a cross. He senses that this is his last chance to destroy the One who is our safe Tower. Satan presses close, speaking lies he hopes will discourage Jesus, urging Him come down from the cross and leave us to our fate.

But Jesus looks ahead. He sees you. He sees me. He sees our fear. Then He voluntarily lays down His life.

From the cradle to the grave, Jesus stood against the gale force of Satanic temptation and human plots. Nothing could destroy the One that God established to be our Tower.

Now He stands beside the throne of God pointing to the nail prints in His hands. The Prince of Peace, the Lamb that was slain, the Mighty King, stands as a safe Tower, pure and glorious amidst the darkness of sin. A Tower built by God and not by humans. A Tower that will never fall.

Whenever I begin a new day or return to the sea I pause and imagine myself enclosed within the safety of my own Tower. I remember that in Him I find everything I will ever need.

Choose Jesus, *your* heart's Mender.

Trust the Tower that will never fall.

Feel the safety of the Tower you run to, not from.

The Spongecola shrimp has its Venus Tower. You have Jesus. Now nothing is left but for you to choose to run to Him.

God saw something else. He saw me living an adventure beyond my wildest dreams.

Lead
Kids to
Jesus

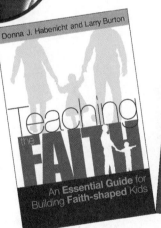

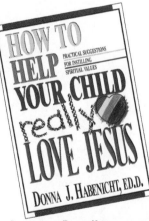

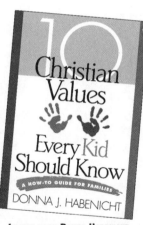

Donna J. Habenicht and Larry Burton

**DONNA HABENICHT & LARRY BURTON
TEACH YOU HOW TO:**

- Help children grow spiritually
- Discipline with grace and love
- Understand the different learning styles
- And much more

0-8280-1819-7

**IN THIS BOOK DONNA HABENICHT
EXPLAINS HOW TO:**

- Peer-pressure-proof your child
- Enhance your child's self-respect
- Understand the different stages of your child's maturity
- Plus so much more

0-8280-1506-6

**IN THIS BOOK DONNA HABENICHT TEACHES
YOU HOW TO:**

- Help children learn to make decisions
- Ways to strengthen family ties
- Help children connect with God through prayer
- And much more

0-8280-0792-6

GIVE YOURSELF
SOMETHING TO LOOK FORWARD TO.

You imagine them somber and reserved. But read their stories, and you'll discover that they were passionate, fascinating, endearing—and not the least bit boring. *Heartwarming Stories of Adventist Pioneers* reveals the personal side of our church leaders. These stories will have you laughing, and crying, and celebrating the God who uses imperfect people to do great things.
Paperback, 0-8280-1895-2.

3 WAYS TO SHOP
- **Visit your local Adventist Book Center®.** • **Call toll-free 1-800-765-6955.**
- **www.AdventistBookCenter.com**

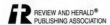

GIVE YOURSELF
SOMETHING TO LOOK FORWARD TO

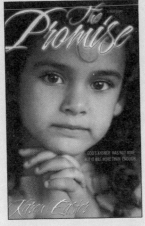

The Promise
Rick, a well-known Christian singer, and Karen, a counselor at a Christian school, are in love—and in trouble. Karen, pregnant out of wedlock, is pressured by Rick to have an abortion, but God makes her an amazing promise. This powerful true story reveals a God who forgives mistakes and offers new beginnings. 0-8280-1886-3. Paperback, 152 pages.

**I'll Hold You
While It Hurts**
Get ready to wipe away the tears as you read these beautiful true stories of children. Each story reminds us that no matter how old—or young—we are, we all need a Savior who will hold us while it hurts. 0-8280-1887-1. Paperback, 144 pages.

3 WAYS TO SHOP
- **Visit your local Adventist Book Center®**
- **Call toll-free 1-800-765-6955**
- **Online at AdventistBookCenter.com**

REVIEW AND HERALD®
PUBLISHING ASSOCIATION